IT'S ALL
ABOUT THE

Accessories

FOR THE WORLD'S
MOST FASHIONABLE DOLLS

1959–1972

Schiffer
Publishing Ltd.®

4880 Lower Valley Road • Atglen, PA 19310

D1568116

2ND EDITION REVISED AND EXPANDED

Other Schiffer Books By The Author:
The Complete & Unauthorized Guide to Vintage Barbie® Dolls With Barbie® & Skipper® Fashions and the Whole Family
978-0-7643-5158-7, $29.99

Other Schiffer Books on Related Subjects:
Coffee with Barbie® Doll, Sandra Bryan 978-0-7643-0412-7, $19.95

Designed by Danielle D. Farmer
Type set in Great Vibes/ITC Bookman/AvantGarde BT

ISBN: 978-0-7643-5135-8
Printed in The United States

Published by Schiffer Publishing, Ltd.
4880 Lower Valley Road
Atglen, PA 19310
Phone: (610) 593-1777; Fax: (610) 593-2002
E-mail: Info@schifferbooks.com
Web: www.schifferbooks.com

For our complete selection of fine books on this and related subjects, please visit our website at www.schifferbooks.com. You may also write for a free catalog.

Schiffer Publishing's titles are available at special discounts for bulk purchases for sales promotions or premiums. Special editions, including personalized covers, corporate imprints, and excerpts, can be created in large quantities for special needs. For more information, contact the publisher.

We are always looking for people to write books on new and related subjects. If you have an idea for a book, please contact us at proposals@schifferbooks.com.

– Dedication –

I dedicate this book to my loving husband, Bill. I appreciate all of his help, support, and patience during the long journey of this book. It is because of him that I know true love; he makes me smile.

Contents

Introduction

– Acknowledgments –

This book would not have been possible if it weren't for the help and support of many special friends. These people let me touch and play with their prized possessions. They let me photograph some wonderful treasures, and their knowledge was priceless.

I thank Susan Anderson of Desperately Seeking Vintage, Sherry Baloun of Gigi's Doll's and Sherry's Teddy Bears, and Bradley Justice of The Swell Doll Shop.

---

*I*n 1959, the Barbie Doll was introduced onto the market and into our hearts. Soon after her friends and family came onto the scene. The fabulous clothes in Barbie's wardrobe were inspired by the latest fashions, some taken straight from the runways of Paris and New York. From head to toe, Barbie, her family, and friends were dressed in outfits that little girls could only dream of. But as little girls grow up and realize the outfits may be wonderful, it is still all about the accessories. Barbie doll had colorful shoes, funky purses, hats, scarves, jewelry, and many accessories. All of these fun items add to the joy of collecting this icon.

This book is about accessories. When a collector today tries to put together an outfit, they soon find out the bulk of the value lies in the shoes, hats, gloves, jewelry, and other important accessories. A missing necklace can sometimes be worth $50, when the total value of the complete outfit is only $75!

This reference guide will aid the collector in identifying and placing his or her accessories with the outfits they belong to. This guide also presents an inclusive library of all the accessories that were available for Barbie, Francie, and all her friends from 1959 to 1972. The book is broken into chapters, each containing a type of accessory, complete with photographs and information on what outfit the accessory came with. Some fun accessories were shared by Barbie, Francie, Skipper, Tutti, and Ken. Those items are cross referenced to help place the accessory with the correct outfit. Some accessories are very rare and seldom seen by collectors. This guide offers pictures of the actual accessory with a detailed description of size, color, and markings. No fakes allowed!

In addition, this guide will also help collectors value their accessories, as it also functions as a complete pricing guide.

Jewelry

One of the most important parts of a young lady's accessories closet is her jewelry box. Early Barbie dolls came with earring holes. Later Mod dolls did not have earring holes, although some of the fashions were still being sold with earrings. Midge, Francie, Julia, Stacey, Jamie, and Skipper never had earring holes at all.

Graduated Pearl Necklace
Can be found with Barbie Golden Girl #911, Barbie Evening Splendour #961, Barbie Gay Parisienne #964, Barbie Easter Parade #971, Barbie Wedding Day Set #972, Barbie Doll Accessories #923, Barbie Sorority Meeting #937, Barbie Belle Dress (pak), Barbie Bride's Dream #947, Barbie Golden Elegance #922, Barbie & Midge Fashion Accents #1880, Barbie Campus Belle (pak), Barbie Wedding Party Gift Set #1017, Barbie Midnight Blue #1617, Barbie Country Club Dance #1627, Barbie On The Avenue #1644, and Finishing Touches (pak).

Double Strand Crystal Bead Necklace, $45
Can be found with Commuter Set #916. (attached strands) and Barbie in Mexico #820 (single long strand).

Crystal Bead Snake Bracelet, $45
Can be found with Commuter Set #916.

Charm Bracelet, $35
Can be found with Barbie Resort Set #963, Barbie Knit Top (pak), Barbie Scoop Neck Playsuit (pak), and Barbie Golden Evening #1610.

Pearl Post Earrings, $15
Can be found with Barbie Evening Splendour #961, Barbie Gay Parisienne #964, Barbie Easter Parade #971, Barbie Wedding Day Set #972, Barbie Sorority Meeting #937, Barbie Brides Dream #947, Barbie Golden Elegance #992, and Barbie & Midge Fashion Accents #1880.

Graduated Pink Pearl Necklace, $45
Can be found with Barbie Plantation Belle #966, Barbie Sophisticated Lady #933, and Barbie Campus Sweetheart #1616.

Pink Pearl Snake Bracelet, $45
Can be found with Barbie Plantation Belle #966.

Pink Pearl Post Earrings, $45
Can be found with Barbie Plantation Belle #966.

Single Pearl Drop Necklace, $65
Can be found with Barbie Suburban Shopper #969, Barbie Roman Holiday #968, Barbie Let's Dance #978, Barbie Swingin' Easy #955, Barbie Busy Morning #956, Barbie Junior Prom #1614, Barbie Fraternity Dance #1638, and Barbie Debutante Ball #1666.

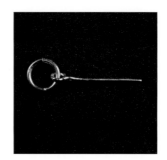

Hoop Earrings, $65
Can be found with Barbie Doll Accessories #923.

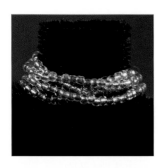

Crystal Bead Four Strand Choker Necklace, $45
Can be found with Barbie Solo In The Spotlight #982.

Three Strand Pearl Necklace Choker with Two Pearl Strand Drops, $75 *(Note: also found with three pearl drops. Not shown.)*
Can be found with Barbie Enchanted Evening #983, Barbie Mood For Music #940, and Accessory Pak (1962).

Four Pearl Drop Earrings, $35
Can be found with Barbie Enchanted Evening #983, Accessory Pak (1962).

Diamond Stud Earrings, $35
Can be found with Barbie Satin Blouse (pak), Barbie Satin n' Rose #1611, and Barbie Sparkling Pink Gist Set.

Pearl Snake Bracelet, $25
Can be found with Barbie Doll Accessories #923 and Accessory Pak (1962).

Gold & Turquoise Bead Necklace, $35
Can be found with Barbie & Midge Fashion Accents #1830 and Barbie Arabian Nights #874.

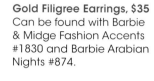

Gold Filigree Earrings, $35
Can be found with Barbie & Midge Fashion Accents #1830 and Barbie Arabian Nights #874.

Gold Snake Bracelet, $25
Can be found with Barbie & Midge Fashion Accents #1830, Barbie Arabian Nights #874.

Turquoise Snake Bracelet, $35
Can be found with Barbie & Midge Fashion Accents #1830 and Barbie Arabian Nights #874.

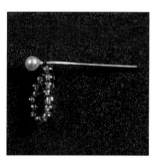

Pearl Post with Crystal Drop Earrings, $45
Can be found with Barbie In Mexico #820.

Red, Black & Crystal Bead Necklace, $35
Can be found with Barbie Sew Free Day n' Night #1723.

Ring on Yellow Satin Pillow, $175
Can be found with Barbie Wedding Party Gift Set #1017.

Pink Snake Bracelet, $35
Can be found with Barbie Sunflower #1683, Barbie & Francie Color Magic Stripes Away #1775, Extra Casuals (pak), and Barbie Evening In #3406.

Hot Pink & Navy Drop Earrings, $45
Can be found with Barbie Sunflower #1683.

Red, Hot Pink & Gold Three Hoop Drop Earrings, $125
Can be found with Barbie Pajama Pow! #1806.

Red Cuff Bracelet, $45
Can be found with Barbie Floating Gardens #1696 and Add-Ons (pak).

Hot Pink Cuff Bracelet, $45
Can be found with Barbie Floating Gardens #1696 and Add-Ons (pak).

Hot Pink Rectangular Drop Earrings, $45
Can be found with Barbie Print Aplenty #1686 and Extra Casuals (pak).

Hot Pink & Red Inter-locking Hoop Earrings, $45
Can be found with Barbie Floating Gardens #1696.

Hot Pink & Green Triangle Drop Earrings, $35
Can be found with Barbie Swirly Cue #1822.

Orange Rectangular Drop Earrings, $35
Can be found with Barbie Zokko! #1820 and All The Trimmings (pak).

Navy & Gold Dot Drop Earrings, $65
Can be found with Barbie Patio Party #1692.

Gold Triangle on Chain Drop Earrings, $25
Can be found with Add-Ons (pak) and Barbie Evening In #3406.

Pink Flower with Gold Bead on Chain Drop Earrings, $45
Can be found with Barbie Romantic Ruffles #1871.

Yellow Flower with Gold Bead on Chain Drop Earrings, $95
Can be found with Barbie Fabulous Formal #1595.

Aqua Butterfly Choker, $45
Can be found with Francie
Pretty Frilly #3366.

**White & Green Bead Double
Strand Necklace, $45**
Can be found with Francie
Tweed-Somes #1286, Add-Ons
(pak), Barbie Terrific Twosome
(pak), and Twiggy Twiggy-Do's
#1725.

Black Butterfly Choker, $145
Can be found with Barbie
Dancing Lights #3437.

**White & Green Bead Single
Strand Necklace, $45**
Can be found with Francie
Tweed-Somes #1286, Barbie
Terrific Twosome (pak), and
Twiggy Twiggy-Do's #1725.

**Hot Pink Wide Choker with
Pink Flower, $95**
Can be found with Barbie
Flying Colors #3492.

Gold Chain Necklace, $95
Can be found with Francie
The Wild Bunch #1766.

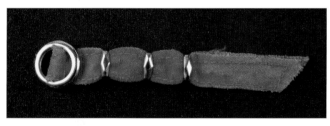

Hot Pink Suede Neck Piece, $75
Can be found with Barbie Fashions N' Sounds Groovin'
Gauchos #1057

**Yellow & Orange Bead Double
Strand Necklace, $35**
Can be found with Barbie
Made For Each Other #1881
and Tour-Ins (pak).

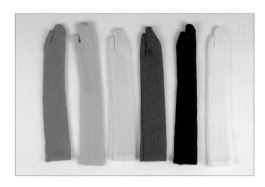

Short White Tricot Gloves, $15
Can be found with Barbie Golden Girl #911, Barbie Commuter Set #916, Barbie Evening Splendour #961, Barbie Plantation Belle #966, Barbie Roman Holiday #968, Barbie Easter Parade #971, Barbie Wedding Day Set #972, Barbie Sheath Sensation #986, Barbie Orange Blossom #987, Barbie Doll Accessories #923, Barbie Garden Party #931, Barbie Golden Elegance #992, Barbie & Midge Costume Completers (pak), Barbie & Midge Going To The Ball (pak), Barbie Campus Belle (pak), Barbie Drum Majorette #875, Barbie Crisp n' Cool #1604, Barbie Garden Tea Party #1606, White Magic #1607, Barbie On The Avenue #1644, Barbie Golden Glory #1645, Barbie Pan American Airways Stewardess #1678, Barbie Fashion Shiner #1691, Barbie Beautiful Bride #1698, Barbie Fancy Trimmings (pak), Barbie Change Abouts (pak), Barbie Fashion Accents #1521, Francie First Formal #1260, Francie Shoppin' Spree #1261, Francie Check This! #1291, Francie Altogether Elegant #1242, Skipper Flower Girl #1904, Skipper Dress Coat #1906, Skipper Outdoor Casuals #1915, Skipper Junior Bridesmaid #1934 and Skipper Velvet n' Lace #1948.

Short Black Tricot Gloves, $45
Can be found with Barbie Black Magic Ensemble #1609, Barbie Lamb n' Leather #1467, Francie Orange Cozy #1263, Francie Two For The Ball #1232, and Skipper Learning To Ride # 1935.

Short Brown Tricot Gloves, $95
Can be found with Barbie Saturday Matinee #1615 and Barbie Riding In The Park #1668.

Short Fuchsia Tricot Gloves, $75
Can be found with Francie The Wild Bunch #1766.

Short Hot Pink Tricot Gloves, $45
Can be found with Barbie Fab City #1874 and Francie Floating-In #1207.

Long Hot Pink Tricot Gloves, $35
Can be found with Barbie Extravaganza #1844.

Long Yellow Tricot Gloves, $75
Can be found with Barbie Regal Red Miss America #3217.

Long Light Pink Tricot Gloves, $35
Can be found with Barbie Sew Free Moonlight n' Roses #1721.

Long Brown Tricot Gloves, $95
Can be found with Barbie Gold n' Glamour #1647.

Long Black Tricot Gloves, $15
Can be found with Barbie Solo In The Spotlight #982, Barbie Career Girl #954, Barbie & Midge Costume Completers (pak), and Barbie Sew Free Debutant Party #1711.

Long White Tricot Gloves, $10
Can be found with Barbie Gat Parisienne #964, Barbie Enchanted Evening #983, Barbie Orange Blossom #987, Barbie Red Flare #939, Barbie Brides Dream #947, Barbie Sophisticated Lady #993, Barbie & Midge Costume Completers (pak), Barbie Cinderella #872, Barbie Wedding Party Gift Set #1017, Barbie Sew Free Day n' Night #1723, Barbie Sew Free Stardust #1722, Barbie Junior Prom #1614, Barbie Campus Sweetheart #1616, Barbie Midnight Blue #1617, Barbie Country Club Dance #1627, Barbie Fraternity Dance #1638, Barbie Holiday Dance #1639, Barbie Fashion Luncheon #1656, Barbie Music Center Matinee #1663, Barbie Debutant Ball #1666, Barbie Benefit Performance #1667, Barbie Here Comes The Bride #1665 and Francie Miss Teenage Beauty #1284.

Red Cotton Mittens, $15
Can be found with Barbie Ski
Queen #948.

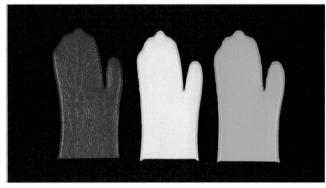

Black Cotton Mittens, $15
Can be found with Ken Ski
Champion #798.

Short Red Plastic Gloves, $15
Can be found with Barbie Winter Holiday #975 and Francie Fur
Out #1262.

Short White Plastic Gloves, $15
Can be found with Barbie Peachy Fleecy #915, Barbie
Commuter Set #916.

Short Blue Plastic Gloves, $95
Can be found with Francie Sportin' Set #1044.

Gold Knit Cotton Mittens, $15
Can be found with Ken Fun On
Ice #791.

Black Leather-like Gloves, $95
Can be found with Ken
Business Appointment #1424.

Light Pink Fleecy Mittens, $35
Can be found with Barbie
Skater's Waltz #1629.

Short Gold Lamé Gloves, $20
Can be found with Barbie Pink
Premiere #1596 and Barbie All
the Trimmings (pak).

Gloves

Brown Plastic Mittens, $65
Can be found with Barbie
Miss Astronaut #1641 and
Ken Mr. Astronaut #1415.

Gray Flocked Plastic Mittens, $95
Can be found with Ken Here Comes
The Groom #1426.

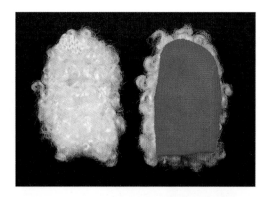

White Plush with Coral Palm Mittens, $20
Can be found with Barbie Skate Mates #1793.

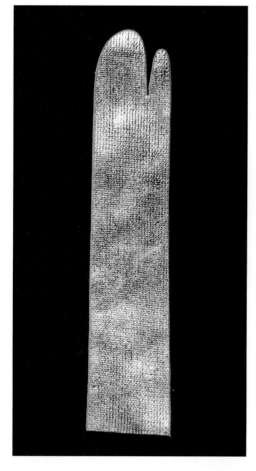

Red Knit With White Fur Mittens, $35
Can be found with Skipper Sledding Fun #1936.

Long Silver Lamé Gloves, $65
Can be found with Barbie Silver
Serenade #3419.

BARBIE & KEN TRAVEL COSTUMES

Brown Felt Hat, $25
Can be found with Ken In Mexico #778.

White Dutch Hat, $20
Can be found with Barbie in Holland #823.

White Eyelet Bonnet Hat, $45
Can be found with Barbie in Switzerland #822.

Black Felt Hat, $25
Can be found with Ken In Switzerland #776.

Blue Felt Hat, $15
Can be found with Ken in Holland #777.

Straw Hat with Flower Trim, $35
Can be found with Ken In Hawaii #1404.

BARBIE & KEN LITTLE THEATER COSTUMES

Red and Black Cap, $15
Can be found with Little Red Riding Hood #880.

Gold Velvet Cap with Feather, $35
Can be found with The Prince #772.

Grandma Night Cap, $15
Can be found with Little Red Riding Hood #880.

Wimple Hat, $20
Can be found with Barbie Guinevere #873.

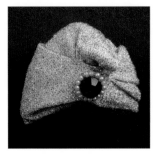

Gold Turban Hat with Jewel, $35
Can be found with Ken Arabian Nights #774.

Silver Plastic Helmet, $20
Can be found with Ken King Arthur #773.

BARBIE HATS

Brown Felt Hat with Feather, $25
Can be found with Barbie Peachy Fleecy Coat #915.

Triple Flower Silk Hat, $95
Can be found with Barbie Commuter Set #916.

Pearl Trimmed Fur Headband Hat, $25
Can be found with Barbie Evening Splendour #961, Barbie Golden Elegance #992, and Barbie and Midge Dress Up Hats (pak).

Black Headband Bow, $275
Can be found with Barbie Easter Parade #971.

Pink and White Picture Hat, $45
Can be found with Barbie Plantation Belle #966.

White Chefs Hat, $15
Can be found with Barbie Q Outfit #962 and What's Cookin? (pak).

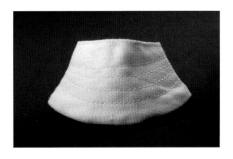

Sailcloth Hat, $15
Can be found with Barbie Resort Set #963.

Straw Cartwheel Hat with Blue Ribbon, $45
Can be found with Barbie Suburban Shopper #969.

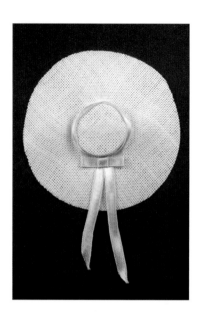

Red Straw Cord Hat Headband, $175
Can be found with Barbie Roman Holiday #968.

Straw Hat with Red Ribbon, $25
Can be found with Barbie Sheath Sensation #986

American Airlines Hat, $25
Can be found with American Airlines Stewardess #984.

Black Felt Mortar Board Hat, $15
Can be found with Barbie Graduation #945 and Ken Graduation #795.

Straw Fishing Hat, $35
Can be found with Picnic Set #967.

Tweed Hat with Satin Red Rose, $25
Can be found with Barbie Career Girl #954.

Straw Hat with Red Scarf, $45
Can be found with Barbie Open Road #985.

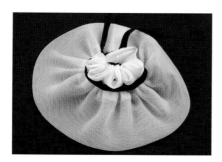

Sheer White Picture Hat, $25
Can be found with Barbie After Five #934 and Barbie and Midge Dress Up Hats (pak).

Blue Tulle Headband Hat, $200
Can be found with Barbie Gay Parisienne #964.

Brown Felt Hat, $25
Can be found with Barbie Sorority Meeting #937.

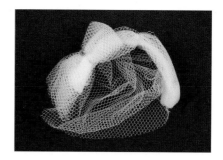

Yellow Tulle Headband Hat, $25
Can be found with Barbie Orange Blossom #987.

Nurse Cap Hat with Blue Trim, $25
Can be found with Barbie Registered Nurse #991.

Yellow Rain Hat, $15
Can be found with Barbie Rain Coat #949 (also called Stormy Weather).

Red Velvet Pillbox Hat, $15
Can be found with Barbie Red Flare #939.

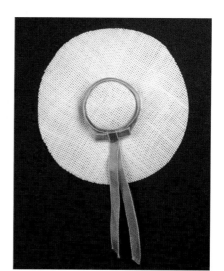

Straw Cartwheel Hat with Red Ribbon, $45
Can be found with Barbie Busy Morning #956.

Black and Yellow Felt Clown Hat, $15
Can be found with Barbie Masquerade #944.

Tan Felt Hat, $15
Can be found with Barbie It's Cold Outside #819.

Brown Tweed Hat, $65
Can be found with Barbie Saturday Matinee #1615.

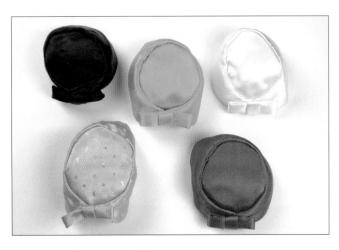

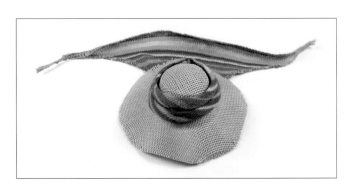

Straw Hat with Knit Scarf, $65
Can be found with Midge Mix n Match Gift set and Barbie Knit Accessories (pak).

Black Satin Pillbox Hat, $45
Can be found with Barbie Satin Bolero (pak).

Green Satin Pillbox Hat, $35
Can be found with Barbie Theatre Date #959 and Barbie and Midge Dress Up Hats (pak).

White Satin Pillbox Hat, $45
Can be found with Barbie Satin Bolero (pak) and Barbie White Magic #1607.

Light Pink with Silver Glitter Satin Pillbox Hat, $35
Can be found with Barbie Satin Bolero (pak) and Barbie Sparkling Pink Gift Set.

Rose Satin Pillbox Hat, $65
Can be found with Barbie Satin Bolero (pak) and Barbie Satin n Rose #1611.

Straw Hat with Blue Scarf, $75
Can be found with Barbie In The Swim (pak).

Straw Hat with Orange Scarf, $75
Can be found with Barbie In The Swim (pak).

Straw Hat with Pink Scarf, $75
Can be found with Barbie In The Swim (pak).

White Cotton Duck Hat, $45
Can be found with Barbie Outdoor Life #1637.

Red Felt Hat, $25
Can be found with Barbie It's Cold Outside #819.

White Nurse Cap Hat, $35
Can be found with Barbie Candy Striper Volunteer #889.

Turquoise Pillbox Hat with Flower Trim, $65
Can be found with Barbie Fashion Editor #1635.

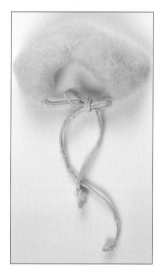

Red Pillbox Hat with Attached Scarf, $65
Can be found with Barbie Matinee Fashion #1640.

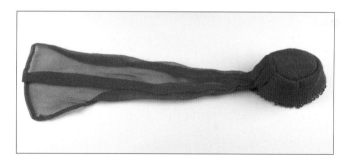

Light Pink Fleecy Muff, $35
Can be found with Barbie Skater's Waltz #1629

Red and White Fur Majorette Hat, $25
Can be found with Barbie Drum Majorette #875.

Gold Tweed Hat with Fur Trim, $75
Can be found with Barbie Gold n' Glamour #1647.

Red Taffeta Hat, $65
Can be found with Barbie and Midge Glamour Hats (pak).

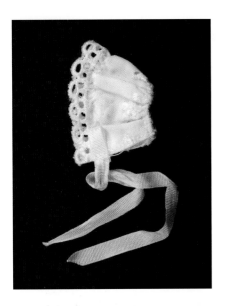

Small White Eyelet Bonnet for Baby, $45
Can be found with Barbie Baby Sits #953 1965 version.

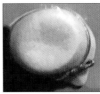

White Felt Hat with Gold Trim, $65
Can be found with Barbie and Midge Glamour Hats (pak).

Felt Hat with Red Band and Bow, $95
Can be found with Barbie Outdoor Art Show #1650.

White Plastic Astronaut Helmet, $45
Can be found with Miss Astronaut #1641.

Black and White Picture Hat, $65
Can be found with Pretty As A Picture #1652.

Pink Satin Hat with White Edging, $65
Can be found with Barbie and Midge Glamour Hats (pak).

Picture Hat with Polka Dots, $65
Can be found with Barbie Lunch On The Terrace #1649.

Blue Taffeta Hat, $95
Can be found with Barbie Reception Line #1654.

White and Silver Picture Hat with Red Roses, $195
Can be found with Barbie Shimmering Magic #1664.

**Light Pink Satin Hat,
$145**
Can be found with
Barbie Fashion
Luncheon #1656.

**Olive Green, Pink, and Orange Head
Scarf, $95**
Can be found with Color Magic Stripes
Away #1775.

**Rose Satin Picture
Hat with Red
Stitching, $150**
Can be found
with Barbie Music
Center Matinee
#1663.

**Blue Gray Twill Pillbox
Hat, $275**
Can be found with
Barbie Pan American
Airways Stewardess
#1678.

Ivory Vinyl Hat, $45
Can be found with
Barbie London Tour
#1661.

Brown Riding Helmet, $45
Can be found with Barbie
Riding In The Park #1668.

**Yellow and Red
Floral Hat, $45**
Can be found
with Barbie Travel
Togethers #1688.

**Yellow and Red Hat with
Black Ties, $35**
Can be found with Barbie
Studio Tour #1690.

Hot Pink Stripe Head Scarf, $145
Can be found with Color Magic Smart Switch #1776.

Yellow Cotton Hood with attached Scarf, $145
Can be found with Barbie The Yellow Go #1816.

Color Block Picture Hat with Blue Ribbon, $145
Can be found with Color Magic Pretty Wild #1777.

Sheer Pink Bonnet with Yellow Ties, $145
Can be found with Color Magic Bloom Burst #1778.

Straw Hat with Yellow Scarf, $45
Can be found with Color Magic Fashion Fun #4041 and Barbie Color Magic Costume Gift Set #1043.

Orange and Hot Pink Vinyl Head Scarf, $25
Can be found with Barbie Drizzle-Dash #1808.

Light Blue Corduroy Bonnet, $25
Can be found with Barbie Now Wow! #1853.

Floral Print Hat, $45
Can be found with Barbie Bermuda Holiday #1810.

Yellow Cotton Hat, $35
Can be found with Barbie Extra-Casuals (pak).

Pink, Burgundy, and Green Hat, $145
Can be found with Barbie Weekenders #1815.

Yellow Plush Hat, $25
Can be found with Barbie Smasheroo #1860.

Green Felt Cowboy Hat, $25
Can be found with Barbie Snap Dash #1824.

White Hat with Plush Crown, $35
Can be found with Barbie Red, White n' Warm #1491.

Aqua Knit Bonnet with Pink Ties, $25
Can be found with Barbie Togetherness #1842.

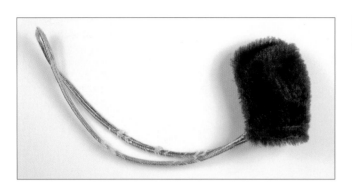

Brown Plush Bonnet, $25
Can be found with Barbie
Winter Wow #1486.

**Yellow Velvet Hat
with Fur Trim, $65**
Can be found with
Julia Candlelight
Capers #1753.

**White Eyelet Hat
with Pink Satin
Trim, $25**
Can be found
with Barbie Midi-
Marvelous #1870.

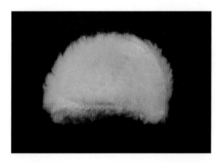

**Green Plush
Hat, $45**
Can be found
with Julia Brrr-
Furrr #1752.

**Orange Plush
Hat, $35**
Can be found
with Barbie Made
For Each Other
#1881 and Jamie
Furry Friends Gift
Set #1584.

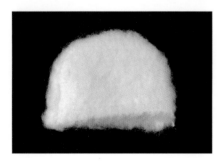

**White Plush Hat,
$125**
Can be found
with Julia Brrr-Furrr
#1752.

**Green Hat with
Blue Band, $20**
Can be found with
Barbie Now Knit
#1452.

Aqua Hat with Yellow Pompon, $35
Can be found with Barbie See-Worthy #1872.

Hot Pink Plush Bonnet with Pink Ties, $45
Can be found with Barbie Action Accents Gift Set #1585.

Yellow Vinyl Hat with Leopard Trim, $20
Can be found with Barbie Great Coat #1459.

Orange Felt Hat with Fringe, $15
Can be found with Barbie Fiery Felt #1789.

White Fur Hat, $45
Can be found with Barbie Lamb n' Leather #1467.

Red Hat with Yellow Fur Trim, $45
Can be found with Barbie Fur Sighted (red version) #1796.

Red Plush Hat, $95
Can be found with Barbie Mad About Plaid Gift Set #1587.

Orange Hat with Yellow Fur Trim, $35
Can be found with Barbie Fur Sighted (orange version) #1796.

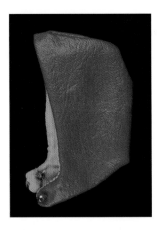

Orange Vinyl Hood, $25
Can be found with Barbie
The Ski Scene #1797.

Coral Nylon Head Scarf, $45
Can be found with Barbie
Fashions n' Sounds Festival
Fashion #1056.

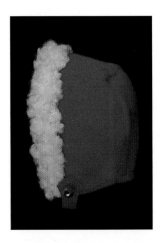

Coral Suede Bonnet, $15
Can be found with Barbie
Skate Mates #1793.

**Red Cotton Hood,
$20**
Can be found
with Barbie Red
For Rain #3409.

**White Plush Hat,
$75**
Can be found with
Barbie Perfectly
Plaid Gift Set #1193.

Plaid Golf Cap, $35
Can be found with
Barbie Golfing
Greats #3413.

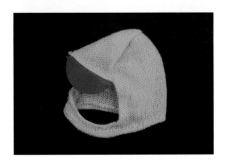

**Yellow Knit Hood
with Orange Visor,
$25**
Can be found with
Barbie Poncho Put-
On #3411.

**Red Suede Hat with
Black Plush Trim, $45**
Can be found with
Barbie Magnificent
Midi #3418.

Beige Crocheted Tam, $65
Can be found with Barbie Fun Fur #3434 and Francie Change Offs #3460.

Olive Knit Cap, $95
Can be found with Barbie Hot Togs #1063.

Orange Felt Gaucho Hat, $45
Can be found with Barbie Goucho Gear #3436.

Multicolor Flannel Hat, $20
Can be found with Barbie Mainly For Rain #3338.

Fuchsia Plush Hood, $25
Can be found with Barbie Soft n' Snug (pak).

Blue Plush Hood, $25
Can be found with Barbie Soft n' Snug (pak).

Red Plush Hood, $25
Can be found with Barbie Soft n' Snug (pak).

Straw Hat with Feather, $25
Can be found with Ken Dreamboat #785 and Ken and Allan Top It Off (pak).

Black and Yellow Felt Clown Hat with Orange Yarn Hair, $20
Can be found with Ken Masquerade #794.

Red Plastic Hunting Cap, $15
Can be found with Ken Hunting Shirt (pak), Ken Going Huntin' #1409 and Ken and Allan Top It Off (pak).

White Surgery Cap, $20
Can be found with Dr. Ken #793.

Red Cap, $15
Can be found with Ken Casuals #782 and Ken Rally Day #788.

Gold Knit Cap, $15
Can be found with Ken Fun On Ice #791 and Ken and Allan Top It Off (pak).

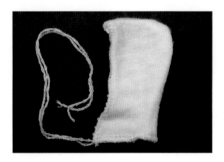

White Skull Cap, $15
Can be found with Ken Masquerade #794.

Red Baseball Cap with "M" on Front, $20
Can be found with Ken Play Ball #792, Ken and Allan Top It Off (pak), and Ricky Little Leaguer #1504.

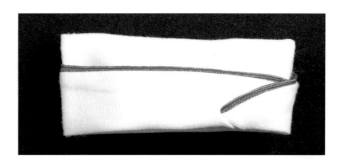

White Cap with Red Edging, $20
Can be found with Ken Fountain Boy #1407.

Red Football Helmet, $15
Can be found with Ken Touchdown #799 and Ken and Allan Sportsman (pak).

White Sailor Cap, $15
Can be found with Ken Sailor #796 and Ken and Allan Top It Off (pak).

Black Knit Ski Cap Hat, $15
Can be found with Ken Ski Champion #798.

Orange Knit Cap, $15
Can be found with Ken Skate Date #1405.

Tan Cap, $15
Can be found with Ken Army and Air Force #797.

Navy Blue Cap, $15
Can be found with Ken Army and Air Force #797.

White Plush Hat with Gold Braid, $25
Can be found with Ken Drum Major #775.

White Chef Hat with Ken's Name on It, $35
Can be found with Ken Cheerful Chef (pak).

Navy American Airlines Cap, $25
Can be found with Ken American Airlines Captain #779.

White Plastic Astronaut Helmet, $65
Can be found with Mr. Astronaut #1415.

White Captain Cap with Black Bill, $125
Can be found with Ken The Yachtsman #789.

Blue and White Houndstooth Cap, $65
Can be found with Ken Holiday #1414.

Gray Plastic Top Hat, $95
Can be found with Ken Here Comes The Groom #1426.

Felt Hat with Black Band, $250
Can be found with Ken Business Appointment #1424.

Fur Black Wig Hat, $175
Can be found with Ken A Go Go #1423.

Yellow and Orange Cap "Twigster" Fabric Hat, $45
Can be found with Ken The Skiing Scene #1438

Red, Yellow, and Blue Knit Cap, $15
Can be found with Ken The Skiing Scene #1438

FRANCIE HATS

Green Knit Cap with Blue Pompon, $20
Can be found with Francie Gad-Abouts #1250.

Blue and White Night Cap, $15
Can be found with Francie Tuckered Out! #1253.

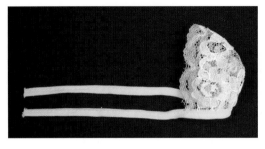

Lace Bonnet with Yellow Ties, $20
Can be found with Francie Fresh As A Daisy #1254.

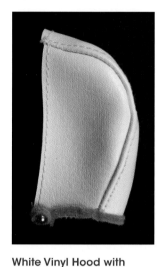

Red Vinyl Bonnet with Yellow Ties, $20
Can be found with Francie Polka Dots & Rain Drops #1255.

Lace Bonnet with Pink Ties, $20
Can be found with Francie Dance Party #1257.

White Vinyl Hood with Pink Trim, $25
Can be found with Francie Leather Limelight #1269.

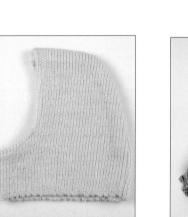

Orange Velour Hood, $65
Can be found with Francie Orange Cozy #1263.

Red Knit Cotton Hood, $65
Can be found with Francie Fur Out #1262.

Yellow Ribbed Knit Cotton Hood, $65
Can be found with Francie Swingin' Skimmy #1264.

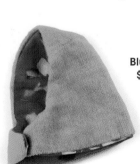

Blue Velvet Hood, $35
Can be found with Francie Style Setters #1268.

Striped Cotton Knit Hood, $65
Can be found with Francie Groovy Get-Up #1270.

Blue and White Floral Cap, $45
Can be found with Francie Bells #1275.

Hot Pink Hat with Flowers, $35
Can be found with Francie Sun Spots #1277.

White Hat with Red Polka Dots and Blue Ribbon, $35
Can be found with Francie Concert In The Park #1256.

Pink and Green Tweed Cap, $125
Can be found with Francie Tweed-Somes #1286.

Navy and White Check Hat, $20
Can be found with Francie Side-Kick #1273.

White Hair Bow, $95
Can be found with Francie Cool White #1280.

Clear Hood with Red Trim, $45
Can be found with Francie Clear Out! #1281.

Yellow Linen Hat, $45
Can be found with Francie Border-Line #1287.

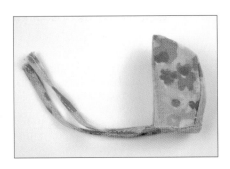

Multicolor Floral Hood, $35
Can be found with Francie In-Print #1293.

White Plush Bonnet, $35
Can be found with Francie Mod-Hatters (pak).

Cotton Denim Cap, $35
Can be found with Francie Denims On! #1290.

Black Plush Bonnet, $35
Can be found with Francie Mod-Hatters (pak).

Orange Suede Hood, $65
Can be found with Francie Furry-Go-Round #1296.

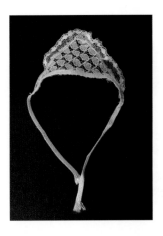

White Lacy Scarf with White Ties, $35
Can be found with Francie Mod-Hatters (pak).

Pink Taffeta Hat, $45
Can be found with Francie Mod-Hatters (pak).

Blue Cotton Hat, $45
Can be found with Francie Mod-Hatters (pak).

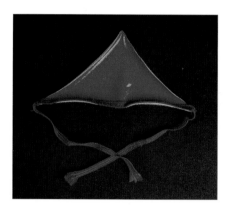

Red Vinyl Scarf Hat, $45
Can be found with Francie Mod-Hatters (pak).

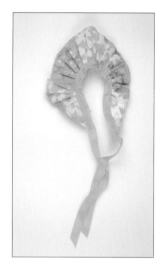

Floral Pleated Head Scarf, $45
Can be found with Francie Tenterrific #1211.

White Satin Hat, $75
Can be found with Francie Culotte-Wot #1214.

Green Floppy Hat, $45
Can be found with Francie Merry-Go-Rounders #1230.

Rose Hat with Blue Ties, $45
Can be found with Twiggy Gear #1728.

White Curly Fur Hat with Green Trim, $35
Can be found with Francie The Combination #1234.

Red Cotton Hat, $25
Can be found with Francie Land Ho! #1220.

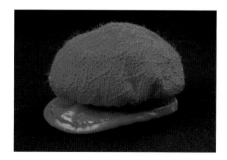

Hot Pink Textured Cap, $45
Can be found with Francie Pink Lightning #1231.

Orange and Yellow Polka Dot Cap $35
Can be found with Francie Slacks n' Cap (pak).

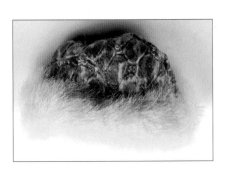

Snakeskin Hat with Yellow Fur Trim, $25
Can be found with Francie Snake Charmers #1245.

Polka Dot Cotton Cap, $35
Can be found with Francie Slacks n' Cap (pak).

Fuchsia Knit Hood with Orange Visor, $45
Can be found with Francie The Wild Bunch #1766.

Zig Zag Cotton Cap, $35
Can be found with Francie Zig Zag Zoom #3445.

Plaid Knit Hat, $35
Can be found Francie Plaid Plans #1767.

Woven Plaid Hat, $150
Can be found with Francie Totally Terrific #3279.

Blue Headband with Red Visor, $75
Can be found with Francie Double Ups #3286.

Floral Cotton Cap, $35
Can be found with Francie Slacks n' Cap (pak).

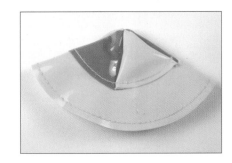

Yellow and Orange Rain Hat, $25
Can be found with Francie Clam Diggers #1258.

36

SKIPPER HATS

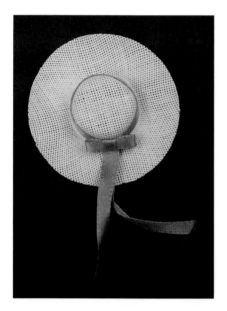

Straw Hat with Red Ribbon, $25
Can be found with Skipper Red Sensation #1901 and Skipper & Skooter Hats n' Hats (pak).

Red Velvet Hat, $15
Can be found with Skipper Dress Coat #1906 and Skipper & Skooter Hats n' Hats (pak).

Pink Hat with Lace Ruffle, $35
Can be found with Skipper & Skooter Hats n' Hats (pak).

Yellow Flower Headband, $25
Can be found with Skipper Flower Girl #1904.

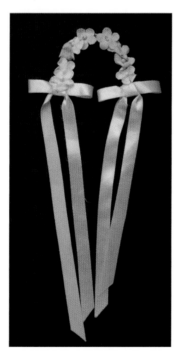

Navy Blue Duck Hat, $15
Can be found with Skipper & Skooter Hats n' Hats (pak).

Pink Flower Headband, $25
Can be found with Skipper Ballet Class #1905.

Yellow and Black Felt Hat with Pompon, $20
Can be found with Skipper Masquerade #1903.

Yellow Cotton Cap, $25
Can be found with Skipper Rain or Shine #1916.

Red Felt Hat with Feather, $45
Can be found with Skipper School Girl #1921.

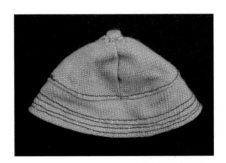

Light Blue Denim Hat, $15
Can be found with Skipper Land and Sea #1917.

White Plush Hood with Ties, $15
Can be found with Skipper Skating Fun #1908.

Straw Hat with Light Blue Ribbon, $45
Can be found with Skipper Happy Birthday #1919.

Red Head Scarf with Polka Dots, $25
Can be found with Skipper Can You Play? #1923.

Houndstooth Hat, $35
Can be found with Skipper Town Togs #1922.

Red Felt Tam Hat, $35
Can be found with Skipper Chill Chasers #1926.

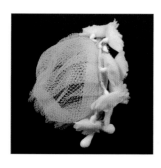

Light Pink Tulle Hat with Pink Flowers, $65
Can be found with Skipper Junior Bridesmaid #1934.

Black Riding Hat, $35
Can be found with Skipper Learning To Ride #1935.

Blue hood with Ties, $25
Can be found with Skipper Sledding Fun #1936.

Floral Hat, $35
Can be found with Skipper Right In Style #1942.

Blue Vinyl Floral Hood, $25
Can be found with Skipper Flower Showers #1939.

Blue Floral Cap, $65
Can be found with Skipper Hearts n' Flowers, blue version #1945.

White Hat with Red Ribbon, $45
Can be found with Skipper All Spruced Up #1941.

Green Floral Cap, $45
Can be found with Skipper Hearts n' Flowers #1945.

White Lace Hood, $35
Can be found with Skipper Popover #1943.

Aqua Riding Cap, $25
Can be found with Skipper Warm n' Wonderful #1959, Skipper Confetti Cutie #1963, and Skipper Happy Times (pak).

Floral Sleep Cap, $15
Can be found with Skipper Jamas n' Jaunties #1944.

Yellow Knit Cap, $25
Can be found with Skipper Side Lights (pak).

Fuchsia Knit Cap, $65
Can be found with Skipper Glad Plaids #1946.

Orange Visor with Blue Scarf and Cinch Ring, $65
Can be found with Skipper Jeepers Creepers #1966.

Orange Felt Cap, $45, with attached Granny Glasses, $95
Can be found with Skipper Skimmy Stripes #1956.

Blue and Pink Knit Headband, $45
Can be found with Skipper Knit Bit #1969.

Orange Cotton Head Scarf, $25
Can be found with Skipper
Pants n' Pinafore #1971.

Yellow Felt Hat, $65
Can be found with Skipper
Twice As Nice #1735.

**Clear Vinyl Hood
with Orange Trim,
$45**
Can be found
with Skipper Drizzle
Sizzle #1972.

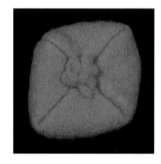

Pink Felt Hat, $25
Can be found with Skipper
Twice As Nice #1735.

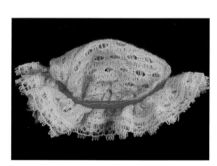

**Yellow Lace Hat,
$25**
Can be found with
Skipper Sunny Suity
#1975.

Pink Cotton Hood, $35
Can be found with Skipper Chilly
Chums #1973.

Blue Knit Cap, $35
Can be found with
Skipper Plaid City
#1977.

**Red Curly Fur Hat,
$35**
Can be found
with Skipper Wooly
Winner #1746.

Aqua Velvet Hood with Ties, $75
Can be found with Skipper Perfectly Pretty #1546.

Red Floral Cap, $15
Can be found with Skipper Super Slacks #1736.

Pink Fur Hat, $35
Can be found with Skipper Pink Princess #1747.

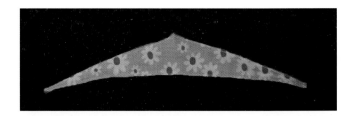

Pink Head Scarf with Flowers $45
Can be found with Skipper Skimmer N' Scarf (pak).

Red Cotton Hat, $25
Can be found with Skipper On Wheels #1032

Multicolor Head Scarf, $65
Can be found with Living Fluff Sunshine Special #1249.

Multi Colored Head Scarf $35
Can be found with Skipper Skimmer N' Scarf (pak).

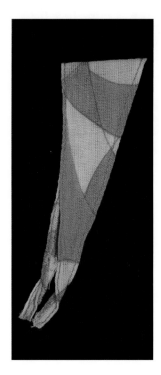

Barbie Pattern Head Scarf $20
Can be found with Skipper Day At The Fair #191

Multicolor Head Scarf (Black Francie Swimsuit Fabric), $65
Can be found with Skipper Triple Treat #1748.

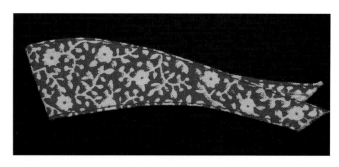

Red and White Floral Head Scarf, $15
Can be found with Skipper Fun Runners #3372.

Pink Velvet Hat with White Trim, $25
Can be found with Skipper Dressed In Velvet #3477.

Multicolor Head Scarf (Barbie Swirly Cue's Fabric), $35
Can be found with Skipper Triple Treat #1748.

Red and White Knit Hat, $25
Can be found with Skipper Long and Short Of It #3478.

White Fur Hood with White Ties, $25
Can be found with Skipper Ice Skatin' #3470.

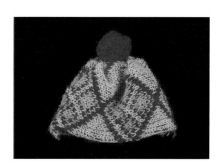

Red and Yellow Knit Hat, $65
Can be found with Skipper Turn Abouts #3295.

TUTTI & TODD

Light Blue Felt Hat, $25
Can be found with Skipper All Over Felt #3476.

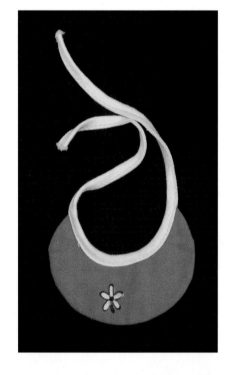

Orange and Yellow Head Scarf, $15
Can be found with Tutti Plantin' Posies #3609.

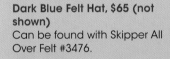

Dark Blue Felt Hat, $65 (not shown)
Can be found with Skipper All Over Felt #3476.

Blue Textured Hat, $15
Can be found with Tutti Puddle Jumpers #3601.

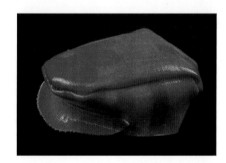

Pink and Red Floral Cap, $45
Can be found with Chris Fun Timers #3301.

White Hat with Red Dots, $20
Can be found with Tutti Sand Castles #3603.

White Hat with Red Pompon, $25
Can be found with Tutti Ship Shape #3602.

Red Hat Box with Lid™, $125
Can be found with Barbie Commuter Set #916.

Green, Blue, and White Hatbox, $25
Can be found with Barbie Travel In Style #1544 and Barbie Tour-Ins (pak).

Red Hat Box with Lid®, $75
Can be found with Barbie Commuter Set #916.

Green and Pink Hatbox with Francie Logo, $65
Can be found with Francie Tweed-Somes #1286 and Francie Partners In Print #1293.

Denim Duffle Bag, $15
Can be found with Ken Sailor #796.

Red, White and Blue Hatbox, $65
Can be found with Shoe Bag #1498 and Francie Clear Out! #1281.

Plaid Overnight Bag, $15
Can be found with Barbie Winter Holiday #975.

American Airlines Flight Bag, $15
Can be found with Barbie American Airlines Stewardess #984 and Ken American Airlines Captain #779.

Red Case with Barbie Face, $35
Can be found with Tutti Let's Play Barbie #3608.

BACKPACKS

Blue and White Backpack with Red Trim, $25
Can be found with Barbie Overall Denim #3488.

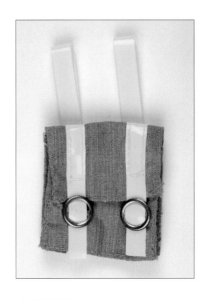

Denim Backpack with Yellow Straps, $35
Can be found with Francie Cool Coveralls #3281.

PURSES & TOTE BAGS

Corduroy Clutch Purse, $25
Can be found with Barbie Golden Girl #911 and Barbie Evening Splendour #961.

Black Shoulder Purse, $15
Can be found with Barbie American Airlines Stewardess #984 and Barbie Pan American Airways Stewardess #1678.

Gold Velvet Clutch Purse, $225
Can be found with Barbie Gay Parisienne #964.

Straw Tote Filled With Fruit, $45
Can be found with Barbie Suburban Shopper #969 and Barbie Busy Morning #956.

Pink Straw Purse, $45
Can be found with Barbie Plantation Belle #966.

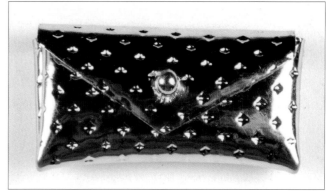

Goldenrod Textured Clutch Purse, $10
Can be found with Barbie Peachy Fleecy #915.

Gold Dimple Clutch Purse, $10
Can be found with Silken Flame #977, Barbie & Midge Fur Stole with Bag (pak), Barbie Party Date #958, Barbie Fashion Accents #1830, Barbie Lamé Sheath (pak), Barbie Knit Dress (pak), Barbie Spectator Sport (pak), Barbie Black Magic #1609, Barbie Country Club Dance #1627, Barbie Holiday Dance #1639, Barbie On The Avenue #1644, Barbie Debutante Ball #1666, Barbie Sunday Visit #1675, and Francie Prom Pinks #1295.

Flower Filled Tote Bag, $15
Can be found with Barbie Doll Accessories #923 and Purse Pak (pak).

Red Velvet Clutch Purse with Diamond Button Closure, $10
Can be found with Barbie Red Flare #939.

Black Clutch Purse, $10
Can be found with Barbie Easter Parade #971, Purse Pak (pak), and Barbie & Midge Costume Completers (pak).

Red Velvet Clutch Purse with Gold Bead Closure, $10
Can be found Purse Pak (pak).

White Clutch Purse, $10 Can be found with Barbie Roman Holiday #968, Barbie Let's Dance #978, Barbie Plain Blouse and Purse (pak), Barbie Swingin' Easy #955, and Barbie & Midge Costume Completers (pak).

Red Clutch Purse, $10
Can be found with Barbie Plain Blouse and Purse (pak) and Barbie & Midge Color Coordinates (pak).

Yellow Clutch Purse, $10
Can be found with Barbie Plain Blouse and Purse (pak) and Barbie & Midge Color Coordinates (pak).

Red Velvet Clutch Purse with White Lining (smaller than pak purse), $35
Can be found with Barbie Golden Elegance #992.

Orange Clutch Purse, $10
Can be found with Barbie & Midge Color Coordinates (pak), Barbie Country Fair #1603 and Francie Wild n' Wooly #1218.

Pink Clutch Purse, $10
Can be found with Barbie Plain Blouse and Purse (pak) and Barbie & Midge Color Coordinates (pak).

Blue Clutch Purse, $10
Can be found with Barbie Plain Blouse and Purse (pak) and Barbie & Midge Color Coordinates (pak).

Stripe Knit Purse, $45
Can be found with Barbie & Midge Knit Accessories (pak) and Midge Mix N' Match Gift Set.

Blue and Red Purse, $10
Can be found with Barbie Sew Free Nine To Five #1701.

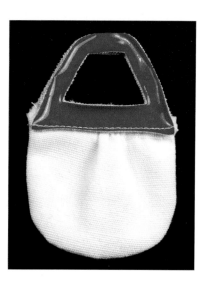

White Purse with Red Handle, $25
Can be found with Barbie Crisp n' Cool #1604.

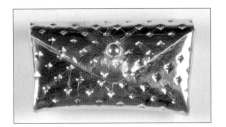

Silver Dimple Clutch Purse, $10
Can be found with Barbie White Magic #1607, Barbie Midnight Blue #1617, Barbie Sparkle Squares #1814, Barbie Extravaganza #1844, Barbie Finishing Touches (pak), Barbie Silver n' Satin #1552, Fashion Accents #1521, and Francie The Silver Cage #1208.

Blue Purse, $10
Can be found with Barbie Sew Free Hootenany #1707.

Beige Purse with Green, Red, and Yellow Detail, $10
Can be found with Barbie Sew Free Pretty Traveler #1706.

Yellow Purse, $15
Can be found with Barbie Sew Free Patio Party #1708.

Turquoise Clutch Purse, $10
Can be found with Barbie Sew Free Day In Town #1712.

Draw String Purse, $15
Can be found with Barbie Sew Free Sightseeing #1713.

Pink Taffeta Purse, $15
Can be found with Barbie Sew Free Moonlight N' Roses #1721.

Small White Vinyl Purse, $20
Can be found with Barbie Sew Free Stardust #1722, Francie Sweet n' Swingin' #1283.

Gold Purse with Fur Trim, $125
Can be found with Barbie Saturday Matinee #1615.

Rust Clutch Purse, $20
Can be found with Barbie Sew Free Golden Ball #1724.

Black Purse, $15
Can be found with Barbie Sew Free Day n' Night #1723.

Olive Tote Purse, $75
Can be found with Barbie Poodle Parade #1643.

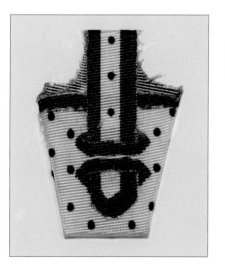

Black and White Purse, $15
Can be found with Barbie Sew Free Day n' Night #1723.

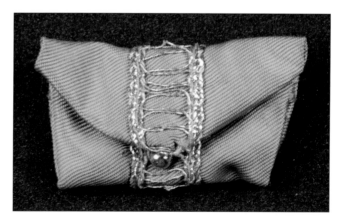

Green Purse with Gold Trim, $95
Can be found with Barbie Golden Glory #1645.

Yellow Tote Color Changing Purse, $45
Can be found with Barbie and Francie Color Magic Fashion Designer Set #4040.

White Purse with Handle, $15
Can be found with Barbie and Midge Match Mates (pak) and Francie Sweet n' Swingin' #1283.

Yellow Sew Free Purse, $25
Can be found with Barbie and Francie Color Magic Fashion Designer Set #4040.

Blue Textured Purse with Handle, $10
Can be found with Barbie and Midge Match Mates (pak), Barbie Fancy Trimmings (pak), and Barbie Change Abouts (pak).

Pink Sew Free Purse, $25
Can be found with Barbie and Francie Color Magic Fashion Designer Set #4040.

Red Shiny Purse, $25
Can be found with Barbie Fashion Shiner #1691.

Red Purse with Handle, $15
Can be found with Barbie and Midge Match Mates (pak), Barbie Fancy Trimmings (pak), and Barbie Change Abouts (pak).

Orange Purse with Handle, $10
Can be found with Barbie and Midge Match Mates (pak).

White with Flower Print Tote Bag, $65
Can be found with Barbie Color Magic Pretty Wild #17.

Multicolored Floral Print Tote Bag, $45
Can be found with Barbie Bouncy-Flouncy #1805.

Ecru Vinyl Purse, $35
Can be found with Barbie London Tour #1661.

Blue Shoulder Bag Purse with Gold Detail, $175
Can be found with Barbie The Yellow Go #1816.

Pink Vinyl Tote with Flower, $15
Can be found with Barbie Extra Casuals (pak), Francie Sun Spots #1277, and Skipper Beachy Peachy #1938.

Blue Clutch Purse, $175
Can be found with Barbie Beautiful Blues #3303.

Silver Purse Lined in Yellow, $65
Can be found with Barbie Fabulous Formal #1595.

Red Vinyl Purse with Gold Button, $35
Can be found with Julia Leather Weather #1751.

Large Pink Purse with Black Trim, $35
Can be found with Barbie Lamb n' Leather #1467.

Silver Purse lined in Pink, $35
Can be found with Barbie Romantic Ruffles #1871.

Purse with Green Vinyl Flap, $45
Can be found with Barbie Mad About Plaid #1587.

Neon Orange Purse with Handle, $15
Can be found with Barbie Tour-Ins and Skipper Trim Twosome #1960.

Pink Suede Shoulder Purse with Fringe, $45
Can be found with Barbie Fashions n' Sounds Groovin' Gauchos #1057.

Pink Satin Purse with Gold Chain, $25
Can be found with Barbie Pink Premiere #1596 and Barbie All The Trimmings (pak).

Multicolored Yarn Shoulder Purse, $75
Can be found with Barbie In Stitches #3432.

Plaid Purse with Orange Vinyl Trim, $25
Can be found with Barbie All About Plaid #3433.

White Textured Clutch Purse, $65
Can be found with Barbie Perfectly Plaid #1193.

Honey Gold Suede Purse with Fringe, $35
Can be found with Barbie Gaucho Gear #3436.

Orange Tote Bag with Flower, $45
Can be found with Barbie Sun Set #1497.

Brown Suede Purse with Attached Belt, $125
Can be found with Barbie Hot Togs #1063.

Gold Satin Purse with Handle, $15
Can be found with Barbie Golden Glitter #3340

Gold Textured Clutch Purse, $45
Can be found with Barbie Regal Red #3217.

Gold Lamé Duffle Bag, $15
Can be found with Barbie
White n' With It #3352.

**Plaid Shoulder Purse with Red
Trim, $25**
Can be found with Barbie
Madras Mad #3485.

**Animal Print Plush Shoulder
Purse, $35**
Can be found with Barbie
Pants-Perfect Purple #3359.

**Yellow Tote Purse with Lace Trim,
$25**
Can be found with Francie
Fresh As A Daisy #1254.

**Red and White
Tweed Clutch
Purse, $25**
Can be found with
Francie Shoppin'
Spree #1261.

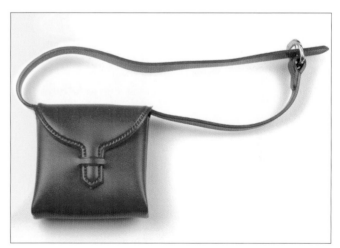

Red Vinyl Shoulder Purse, $35
Can be found with Francie
Check Mates #1256 and
Francie Bells #1275.

**White Purse with Red Dots
and Red Handle, $25**
Can be found with Francie
Concert In The Park #1256.

Red Shoulder Purse, $45
Can be found with Francie Bells #1275, Skipper Wooly Winner
#1746.

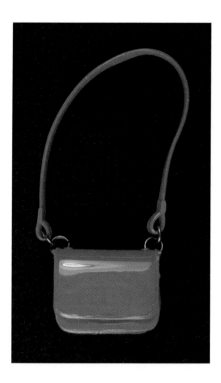

Orange Shoulder Purse, $25
Can be found with Francie Mini-Chex #1209 and Francie Wild n' Wooly #1218.

Yellow Drawstring Tote, $35
Can be found with Francie Summer Coolers #1292.

Orange Drawstring Purse with Yellow Ties, $45
Can be found with Francie Olde Look #3458.

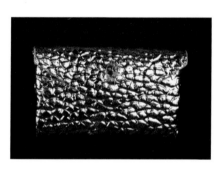

Silver Textured Clutch Purse, $35
Can be found with Francie Altogether Elegant #1242 and Francie Twilight Twinkle #3459.

White Tote with Green Trim, $35
Can be found with Francie Tenterrific #1211.

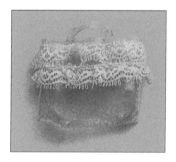

Clear Purse Tote with White Lace Trim, $35
Can be found with Francie Sugar Sheers #1229.

Yellow Shoulder Purse with Chain, $65
Can be found with Twiggy Twiggy-Do's #1725.

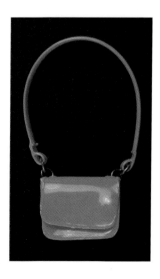

Pink Shoulder Purse, $15
Can be found with Francie Sissy Suits #1228 and Chris Fun Timers #3301.

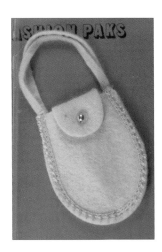

Gold Felt Purse, $25
Can be found with Francie
Western Wild (pak).

Yellow Suede Purse, $25
Can be found with Francie
Western Wild (pak).

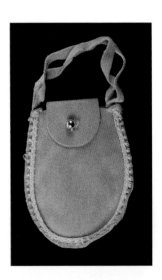

Aqua Suede Purse, $25
Can be found with Francie
Western Wild (pak).

White Suede Purse, $25
Can be found with Francie
Western Wild (pak).

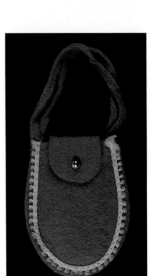

Brown Suede Purse, $25
Can be found with Francie
Western Wild (pak).

Purple Felt Purse, $25
Can be found with Francie
Western Wild (pak).

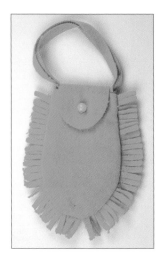

**Aqua Suede Purse with Fringe,
$35**
Can be found with Buckaroo
Blues #3449.

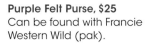

Yellow Shoulder Purse with Clasp and Gold Button, $145
Can be found with Francie Suited For Shorts #3283.

Navy Suede Shoulder Purse with Red Trim, $125
Can be found with Francie Double Ups #3286.

Navy and White Check Purse with Apple Decal, $65
Can be found with Francie Checker Chums #3278.

Yellow Shoulder Purse with Orange Trim, $45
Can be found with Francie The Slacks Suit #3276.

Yellow Shoulder Purse with Gold Button, $145
Can be found with Francie Totally Terrific #3279.

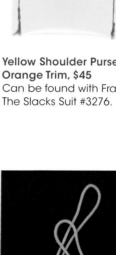

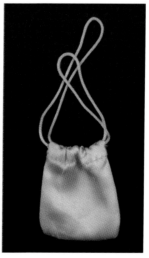

Red Floral Print Purse, $35
Can be found with Francie Right For Stripes #3367.

Pink Satin Drawstring Slipper Bag, $10
Can be found with Barbie Ballerina #989 and Skipper Ballet Class #1905.

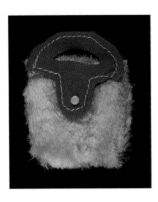

Light Blue Fuzzy Purse with Rose Trim, $145
Can be found with Francie Smashin' Satin #3287.

Aqua Blue, Pink, and Green Tote Bag, $35
Can be found with Skipper Country Picnic #1933.

Red Velvet Purse with Gold Handle, $10
Can be found with Skipper Dress Coat #1906.

Red Suede Purse with Gold Chain, $45
Can be found with Francie Red, White & Bright #3368.

White Shoulder Purse with Red Trim, $45
Can be found with Skipper All Spruced Up #1941.

Yellow Shoulder Purse, $45
Can be found with Skipper Hearts n' Flowers #1945.

Rainbow Purse, $25
Can be found with Skipper Sunny Pastels #1910.

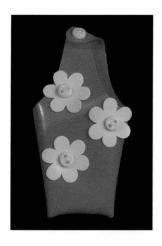

Pink Tote with Yellow Flowers, $15
Can be found with Skipper Fancy Pants #1738 and Skipper Side Lights (pak).

Aqua Satin Drawstring Slipper Bag, $20
Can be found with Skipper Ballerina #3471.

Plaid Shoulder Purse with Gold Chain, $55
Can be found with Skipper Glad Plaids #1946.

Yellow Felt Shoulder Purse, $65
Can be found with Skipper All Over Felt #3476.

White Shoulder Purse with Gold Trim and Gold Chain, $15
Can be found with Skipper White, Bright n' Sparkling #3374.

Red Shoulder Bag with Yellow Striped Handle, $65
Can be found with Skipper Turn Abouts #3295.

Cummerbunds

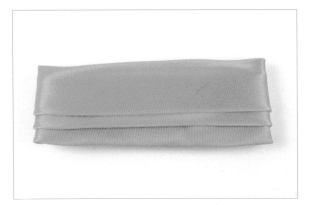

Green Satin Cummerbund, $35
Can be found with Ken In Mexico #778.

Burgundy Satin Cummerbund, $15
Can be found with Ken Tuxedo #787.

Red Satin Cummerbund, $95
Can be found with Ken Best Man #1425.

Light Burgundy Satin Cummerbund, $15
Can be found with Ken the Night Scene #1496.

Shiny White Belt, $25
Can be found with Barbie Cruise Stripes #918 and Roman Holiday #968.

Hot Pink Vinyl Belt, $25
Can be found with Barbie Slacks (pak), Barbie Learns to Cook #1634 and Barbie Lunchtime #1673.

Orange Vinyl Belt, $25
Can be found with Barbie Slacks (pak).

Blue Vinyl Belt, $25
Can be found with Barbie Slacks (pak).

Yellow Vinyl Belt, $25
Can be found with Barbie Slacks (pak).

Red Vinyl Belt, $25
Can be found with Barbie Slacks (pak).

Navy Blue Straw Belt, $25
Can be found with Barbie Busy Gal #981.

Gold Dimple Wide Belt, $15
Can be found with Barbie Silken Flame #977, Barbie Party Date #958, Barbie Golden Evening #1610, and Barbie Glimmer Glamour #1547.

White Vinyl Belt, $15
Can be found with Barbie Winter Holiday #975.

Gold Cord Belt, $25
Can be found with Barbie Gold Knit Dress (pak), Spectator Sport (pak).

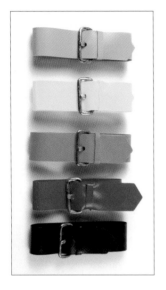

Blue Wide Vinyl Belt, $25
Can be found with Barbie
Scoop Neck Playsuit (pak).

Yellow Wide Vinyl Belt, $25
Can be found with Barbie
Scoop Neck Playsuit (pak).

Orange Wide Vinyl Belt, $25
Can be found with Barbie
Scoop Neck Playsuit (pak).

Red Wide Vinyl Belt, $25
Can be found with Barbie
Scoop Neck Playsuit (pak).

Black Wide Vinyl Belt, $25
Can be found with Barbie
Scoop Neck Playsuit (pak).

Blue Cord Belt, $35
Can be found with Barbie Blue
Knit Dress (pak) and Spectator
Sport (pak).

Yellow Cotton Belt, $15
Can be found with Barbie
Rain Coat (also called Stormy
Weather) #949 and Skipper
Rain or Shine #1916.

**Red Felt Belt with Large
Button, $20**
Can be found with Barbie It's
Cold Outside #819.

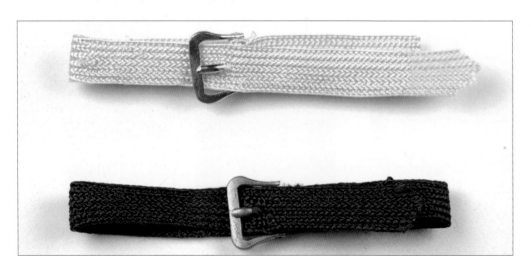

Tan Belt, $15
Can be found with Ken Army
and Air Force #797.

Navy Belt, $15
Can be found with Ken Army
and Air Force #797.

Red Cord Belt, $25
Can be found with Barbie Stripe Knit Dress (pak) and Spectator Sport (pak)

Tan Felt Belt with Large Button, $15
Can be found with Barbie It's Cold Outside #819.

Blue Cotton Sash with Fringe, $25
Can be found with Barbie Knit Separates #1602 and Knit Skirt (pak).

Courtesy of Marl & B

Gold Cotton Sash with Fringe, $25
Can be found with Barbie Knit Skirt (pak).

Courtesy of Marl & B

Stripe Cotton Sash with Fringe, $25
Can be found with Barbie Knit Skirt (pak).

Black Felt Corset with Yellow Ties, $35
Can be found with Barbie Little Red Riding Hood and The Wolf #880.

Green Felt Corset, $35
Can be found with Barbie In Switzerland #822.

Large Silver Chain Belt, $25
Can be found with Barbie Guinevere #873.

Gold Belt, $35
Can be found with Ken
King Arthur #773.

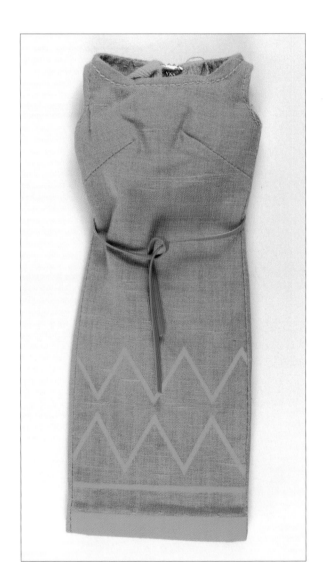

White Belt with Gold Trim, $25
Can be found with Ken Arabian Nights #774.

Green Vinyl Tie Belt, $95
Can be found with Barbie Junior Designer #1620.

Gold Belt with Oval Gold Buckle, $125
Can be found with Barbie Hostess Set #1034.

Light Pink Vinyl Belt, $45
Can be found with Barbie Dancing Doll #1626.

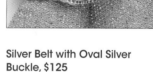

Silver Belt with Oval Silver Buckle, $125
Can be found with Barbie Invitation To Tea #1632.

Red Vinyl Belt with Square Buckle, $45
Can be found with Barbie Hostess Set #1034, Barbie Student Teacher #1622, and Barbie Aboard Ship #1631.

Gold Belt with Square Gold Buckle, $65
Can be found with Barbie Intrigue #1470.

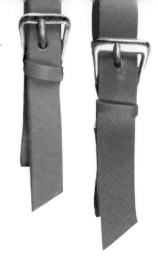

Hot Pink Stripe Belt, $65
Can be found with
Barbie Color Magic
Smart Switch #1776.

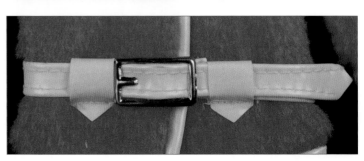

**Vinyl Belt with Rectangular
Buckle, $35**
Can be found with Barbie
Snug Fuzz #1813.

**Extra Long Silver Belt with
Round Buckle, $95**
Can be found with Barbie
Silver n' Satin #1552.

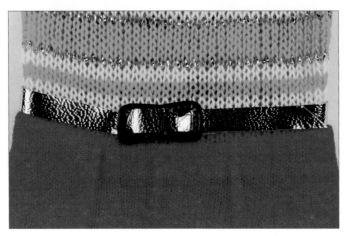

Thin Gold Belt, $65
Can be found with Barbie
Team-Ups #1855.

Gold Chain Belt with Hook Closure, $45
Can be found with Barbie Smasheroo #1860 and
Skipper Confetti Cutie #1963.

**Gold Chain Belt with Gold
Disc, $35**
Can be found with Barbie Shift
Into Knit #1478 and All The
Trimmings (pak).

Wide Gold Belt with Square Buckle, $35
Can be found with Barbie Winter Wow #1486.

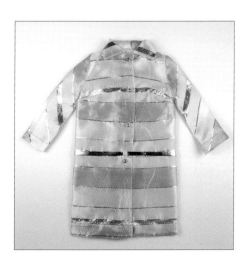

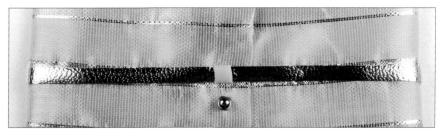

Thin Gold Belt, $75
Can be found with Barbie All That Jazz #1848.

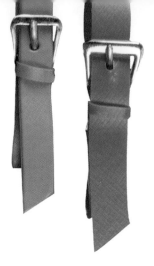

Wide Silver Belt with Round Buckle, $25
Can be found with Barbie Finishing Touches (pak) and Fashion Accents #1521 (pak).

Gold Chain with Detailed Clasp, $45
Can be found with Barbie Plush Pony #1873 and Skipper Side Lights (pak).

Silver Attached Belt with Buckle, $45 (price includes dress)
Can be found with Barbie Now Knit #1452.

White Textured Vinyl Belt with Oval Gold Buckle, $35
Can be found with Barbie Red, White n' Warm #1491.

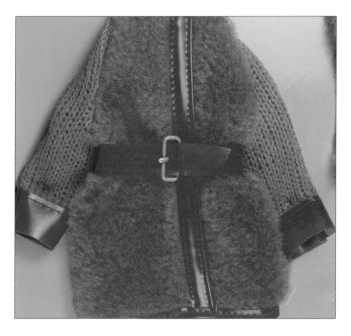

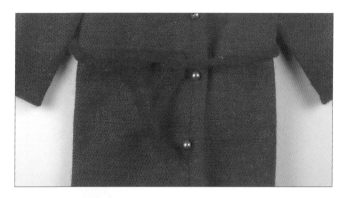

**Orange Attached Yarn Belt,
$15 (price includes coat)**
Can be found with Barbie Anti-
Freezers #1464.

Hot Pink Wide Hot Pink Attached Belt, $65 (price includes coat)
Can be found with Jamie Furry Friends #1584.

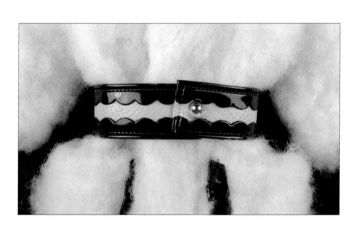

**Black and Pink Vinyl Belt,
$45**
Can be found with Barbie
Lamb n' Leather #1467.

**Green Attached Vinyl
Belt, $125 (price includes
dress)**
Can be found with Barbie
Mad About Plaid #1587.

**Gold Chain
Belt with Red
Flower, $45**
Can be
found with
Important
Investment
#1482.

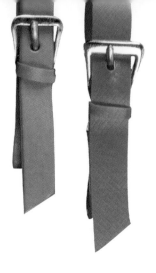

**Pink Vinyl Belt with Oval Buckle,
$45**
Can be found with Barbie
Ruffles n' Swirls #1783 and
Francie Midi Bouquet #3446.

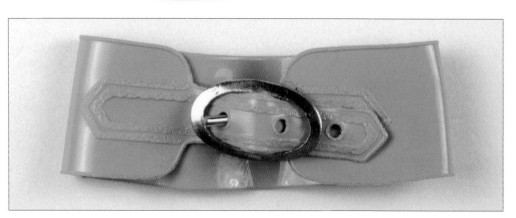

**Gold and Silver Braid Belt,
$20**
Can be found with Barbie
Harem-m-m's #1784.

Aqua Vinyl Belt, $25
Can be found with Barbie Mood Matchers #1792.

Blue Foil Attached Belt, $95 (price includes coat)
Can be found with Barbie Maxi n' Mini #1799.

Orange Vinyl Belt with Round Buckle, $25
Can be found with Barbie Made For Each Other #1881.

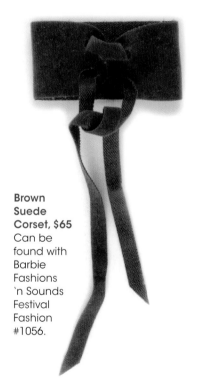

Brown Suede Corset, $65
Can be found with Barbie Fashions 'n Sounds Festival Fashion #1056.

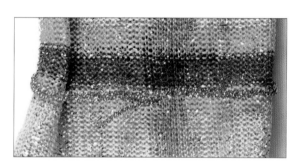

Thin Double Strand Attached Gold Belt, $65 (price includes dress)
Can be found with Barbie Maxi n' Mini #1799.

Red Cotton Attached Belt with Gold Buckle, $25 (price includes coat)
Can be found with Barbie Red For Rain #3409.

Satin Blue Belt with Nylon Trim, $25
Can be found with Barbie Satin Slumber #3414.

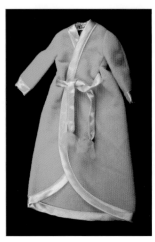

White Wide Textured Belt, $45
Can be found with Barbie Wild n' Wintery #3416.

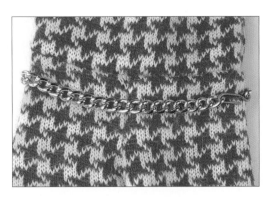

Gold Chain Attached Belt, $35
(price includes jumpsuit)
Can be found with Barbie Poncho Put-On 3411.

Purple Suede Belt with Foil Backing, $45
Can be found with Barbie Bubbles n' Boots #3421.

Purple Suede Belt with Open Dots, $45
Can be found with Barbie Night Lighter #3423

Orange Suede Belt with Silver Buckle, $45
Can be found with Barbie Turtle n' Tights #3426.

Blue Satin Attached Tie Belt, $35 (price includes robe)
Can be found with Barbie The Dream Team #3427.

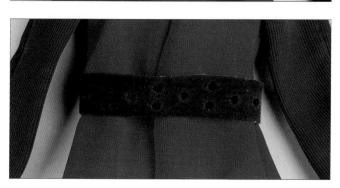

Royal Blue Textured Belt, $175
Can be found with Barbie Wild Things #3439.

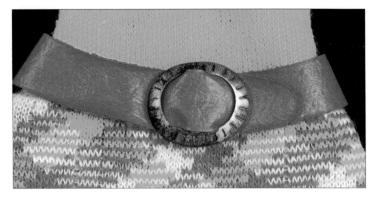

Orange Vinyl Attached Belt, $45 (price includes dress)
Can be found with Barbie All About Plaid #3433.

Brown Suede Belt with Attached Bag, $125
Can be found with Barbie Hot Togs #1063.

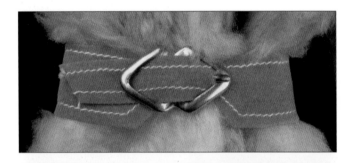

Extra Long Red Vinyl Belt with Square Buckle, $25
Can be found with Barbie Furry n' Fun #3336.

Honey Gold Suede Belt, $45
Can be found with Barbie Fun Fur #3434.

Black Textured Tie Belt, $65
Can be found with Francie
Fur Out #1262.

**Gold Belt with Square Buckle,
$65**
Can be found with Barbie
Regal Red #3217 and Francie
Prom Pinks #1295.

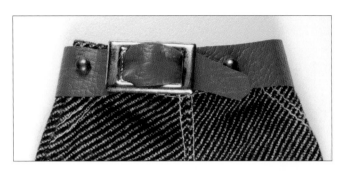

Brown Vinyl Belt with Square Buckle and Gold Studs, $15
Can be found with Barbie Good Sports #3351.

Double Gold Chain Belt with Hook Closure, $45
Can be found with Barbie Pants-Perfect Purple #3359

Red Vinyl Belt with Pockets, $65
Can be found with Barbie The Short Set #3481.

Black Velvet Corset, $35
Can be found with Barbie Pleasantly Peasanty #3360.

Thin Yellow Vinyl Belt with Gold Buckle, $45
Can be found with Francie Hip Knits #1265.

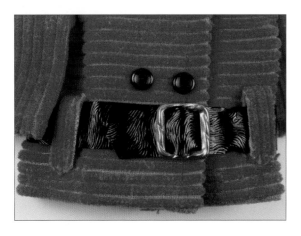

Black Textured Wide Belt, $45
Can be found with Francie Groovy Get-Up #1270.

Gold Belt with Gold Buckle, $45
Can be found with Francie Go Gold #1294.

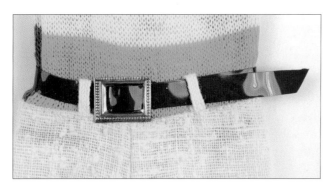

Navy Blue Shiny Belt with Gold Buckle, $25
Can be found with Francie Denims On #1290, Casey Goes Casual $3304, and Twiggy Gear #1728.

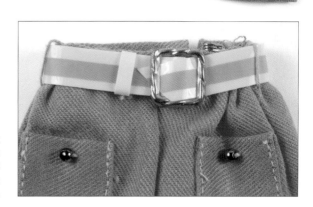

Yellow and Pink Striped Vinyl Belt with Gold Buckle, $45
Can be found with Francie Sissy Suits #1228.

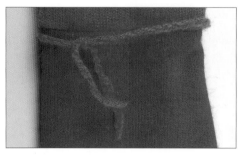

Orange Yarn Attached Tie Belt, $95 (price includes dress)
Can be found with Francie The Wild Bunch #1766.

Aqua Satin Belt, $35
Can be found with Francie Satin Supper #3443.

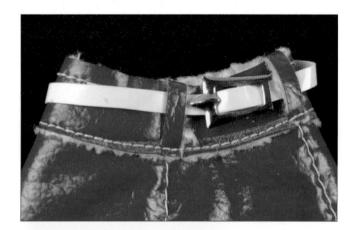

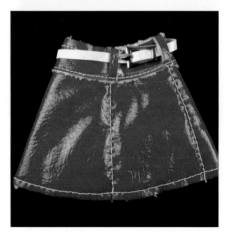

Thin White Vinyl Belt with Silver Buckle, $45
Can be found with Francie Long On Leather #1769.

Blue Textured Belt with Round Buckle, $45
Can be found with Francie Zig Zag Zoom #3445.

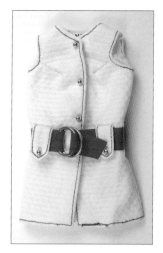
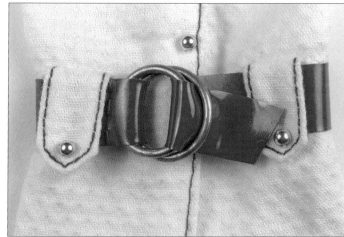

Red Wide Belt with Gold Rings, $35
Can be found with Francie With It Whites #3448.

White Belt with Round Gold Buckle, $25
Can be found with Francie Little Knits #3275.

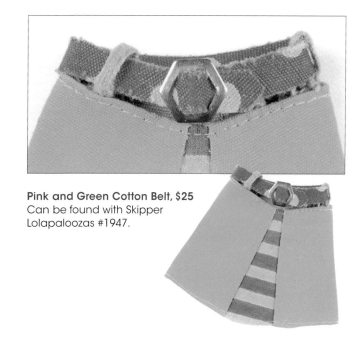

Pink and Green Cotton Belt, $25
Can be found with Skipper Lolapaloozas #1947.

Brown Vinyl Belt with Oval Buckle, $15
Can be found with Francie Ready! Set! Go! #3365.

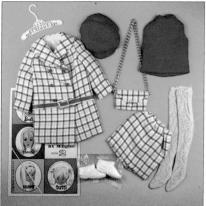

Pink and Yellow Vinyl Belt, $35
Can be found with Skipper Glad Plaid #1946.

Green Felt Belt with Gold Buckle, $15
Can be found with Skipper Town Togs #1922.

Blue and Pink Floral Vinyl Belt, $15
Can be found with Skipper Flower Showers #1939.

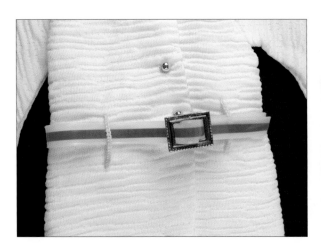  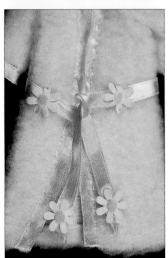

Extra Long White and Orange Vinyl Belt with Gold Buckle, $25
Can be found with Skipper Trim Twosome #1960.

Yellow Satin Belt With Large Daisies, $20
Can be found with Skipper
Came with either large or small
flowers. Lemon Fluff #1749.

Hot Pink Plastic Chain Belt, $25
Can be found with Skipper Real Sporty #1961 and Skipper Side Lights (pak).

Red Vinyl Belt with Gold Buckle, $15
Can be found with Skipper Patent n' Pants #1958.

Pink and Yellow Vinyl Belt, $15
Can be found with Skipper Hopscotchins #1968, Skipper Side Lights (pak).

Blue Knit Belt, $25
Can be found with Skipper Knit Bit #1969.

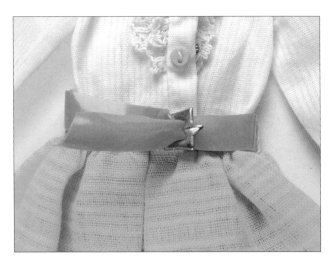

Pink Vinyl Belt with Gold Buckle, $15
Can be found with Skipper Ice Cream n' Cake #1970.

Pink Cotton Belt, $25
Can be found with Skipper Chilly Chums #1973.

Yellow, Pink, and White Attached Belt, $35 (price includes dress)
Can be found with Skipper Daisy Crazy #1732.

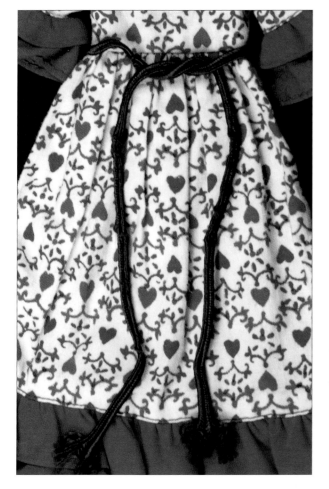

Navy Blue Tie Belt, $35
Can be found with
Skipper Red, White n'
Blues #3296.

Red Vinyl Belt with Gold Buckle, $15
Can be found with Skipper Fun Runners #3372.

**Red Velveteen Belt with
Black Ties, $15**
Can be found with Skipper
Flower Power #3373.

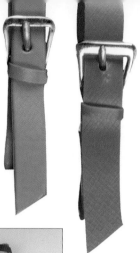

Burgundy Vinyl Belt, $25
Can be found with Ken Shore Lines #1435 and Ken Bold Gold #1436.

Extra Long Blue Belt with Gold Buckle, $25
Can be found with Skooter Cut N' Button Costumes #1036.

Yellow Vinyl Belt, $25
Can be found with Skipper Summer Slacks (pak) and Skipper Side Lights (pak).

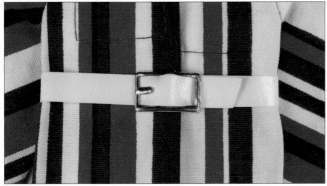

White Vinyl Belt, $15
Can be found with Ken The Casual Scene #1472.

Brown Suede Belt, $10
Can be found with Ken Way Out West #1720.

Brown Suede Belt, $10
Can be found with Ken The Suede Scene #1439.

Blue Belt with Triangle Buckle, $15
Can be found with Ken Casual Cords #1717.

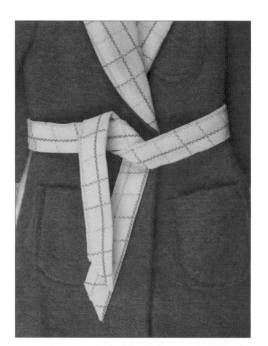

Yellow Cotton Tie Belt, $15
Can be found with Ken
Breakfast At 7 #1428.

Red and White Vinyl Belt, $45
Can be found with Ken Red,
White & Wild #1829.

Burgundy Vinyl Belt, $65
Can be found with Ken Mod
Madras #1828.

Red and White Potholder, $10
Can be found with Barbie-Q Outfit #962, Apron and Utensils (pak) and What's Cookin? (pak).

Metal Spatula with Red Handle, $8
Can be found with Barbie-Q Outfit #962, Apron and Utensils (pak), What's Cookin? (pak), Ken Cheerful Chef (pak), and Tutti Sand Castles #3603.

Pink, Blue, and Red Barbie Print Potholder, $35
Can be found with Barbie Learns To Cook #1634.

Metal Spoon with Red Handle, $8
Can be found with Barbie-Q Outfit #962, Apron and Utensils (pak), What's Cookin? (pak), Ken Cheerful Chef (pak), Barbie and Francie Color Magic Fashion Fun #4041, and Skipper Cookie Time #1912.

Red, Blue, and Green Barbie Print Potholder, $65
Can be found with Barbie's Hostess Set #1034.

Metal Knife with Red Handle, $8
Can be found with Barbie-Q Outfit #962, Apron and Utensils (pak), and What's Cookin? (pak).

Red and White Oven Mitt, $35
Can be found with Ken Cheerful Chef (pak).

Metal Knife with Raised Detail on Handle, $25
Can be found with Barbie Candy Striper Volunteer #889. also found with Hostess Set #1035.

Metal Fork with Raised Detail on Handle, $25
Can be found with Barbie Candy Striper Volunteer #889. also found with Hostess Set #1035.

Metal Spoon with Raised Detail on Handle, $25
Can be found with Barbie Candy Striper Volunteer #889. also found with Hostess Set #1035.

Metal Fork with Hot Dog, $45
Can be found with Ken Cheerful Chef (pak) and Skipper Country Picnic #1933.

Metal Spoon, $25
Can be found with Barbie Registered Nurse #991, Ken Doctor Kit (pak), Barbie Have Fun (pak), Ken Fountain Boy #1407, Barbie and Midge Set n' Serve (pak), Francie Dance Party #1257, Skipper Tea Party #1924, Skipper Posy Party #1955, and Tutti and Todd Sundae Treat #3556.

Wooden Rolling Pin with Red Handles, $8
Can be found with Barbie-Q Outfit #962, Apron and Utensils (pak), What's Cookin? (pak), and Skipper Cookie Time #1912.

Red Apple Made of Wax, $20
Can be found with Barbie Sweet Dreams #973, Ken Doctor Kit (pak), and Skipper School Girl #1921.

Honey Bun with Icing Made of Wax, $15
Can be found with Ken Sleeper Set #781 and Ken Sleeper Set #782.

Watermelon Slice Made of Wax, $35
Can be found with Barbie Candy Striper Volunteer #889 and Skipper Country Picnic #1933.

Six Rolls Made of Wax, $45
Can be found with Barbie Little Red Riding Hood and The Wolf #880.

Slice of White Toast, $45
Can be found with Barbie Kitchen Magic (pak).

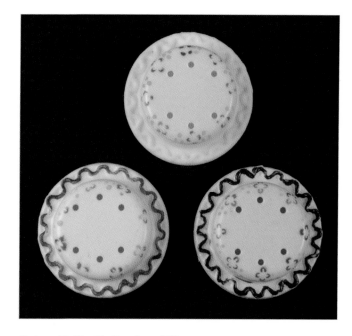

Slice of Brown Toast, $15
Can be found with Barbie's Hostess Set #1034, Barbie Learns To Cook #1634, Barbie Lunchtime #1673, and Barbie Cook-Ups (pak).

Cake with Vanilla Frosting, $15
Can be found with Skipper Happy Birthday #1919.

Cake with Milk Chocolate Frosting, $15
Can be found with Barbie's Hostess Set #1034 and Skipper Happy Birthday #1919.

Cake with Dark Chocolate Frosting, $15.
Can be found with Barbie's Hostess Set #1034 and Skipper Happy Birthday #1919.

Plastic Hamburger, $15
Can be found with Barbie Sun Set Accessories #1497 and Skipper Country Picnic #1933.

Pink Cotton Candy, $35
Can be found with Barbie Fun At The Fair, #1624.

Plastic Pineapple, $15
Can be found with Barbie In Hawaii #1605.

Ice Cream Cone, $25
Can be found with Skipper Country Picnic #1933.

Cola Soda with Straw, $65
Can be found with Barbie
Friday Night Date #979.

**Chocolate Soda with Straw,
$25**
Can be found with Barbie
Have Fun (pak) and Ken
Fountain Boy #1407.

Orange Soda with Straw, $20
Can be found with Leisure
Hours (pak), Barbie Friday
Night Date #979, and Barbie
Candy Striper Volunteer #889.

**Strawberry Soda with Straw,
$25 (without straw, $20)**
Can be found with Barbie
Have Fun (pak), Ken Fountain
Boy #1407, and Skipper
Country Picnic #1933.

**Slice of Cake with Strawberry
Filling, $45**
Can be found with Tutti Birthday
Beauties #3617.

Glass of Milk, $20
Can be found with Ken Sleeper
Set #781, Ken Sleeper Set #782,
Ken Doctor Kit (pak), and Ken
Off To Bed #1413.

**Slice of Cake with Strawberry
Filling, $45**
Can be found with Barbie's
Hostess Set #1034, Skipper Tea
Party #1924, and Tutti Birthday
Beauties #3617.

Black Serving Tray, $15
Can be found with Leisure
Hours (pak) and Barbie Friday
Night Date #979.

**Black Serving Tray with Flat
Handles, $65**
Can be found with Barbie
Friday Night Date #979.

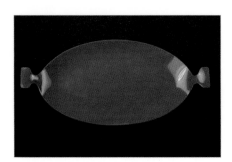

**Brown Serving
Tray, $25**
Can be found
with Barbie Have
Fun (pak) and
Ken Fountain Boy
#1407.

Silver Serving Tray, $65
Can be found with Barbie's Hostess Set #1034.

Blue Bowl with Flowers, $45 (picture shown with replaced flowers)
Can be found with Barbie's Hostess Set #1034.

White Serving Tray, $45
Can be found with Barbie Candy Striper Volunteer #889.

Aqua Tea Cup and Saucer, $35
Can be found with Barbie and Midge Set n' Serve (pak), Barbie Cook-Ups (pak), and Skipper Tea Party #1924.

Blue Plate with Raised Floral Design, $25
Can be found with Barbie Candy Striper Volunteer #889 and Skipper Country Picnic #1933.

Pink Tea Cup with Saucer, $45
Can be found with Barbie's Hostess Set #1034 and Barbie Invitation To Tea #1632.

Pink Plate, $35
Can be found with Barbie's Hostess Set #1034 and Tutti Birthday Beauties #3617.

Aqua Plate, $25
Can be found with Barbie and Midge Set n' Serve (pak), Barbie Cook-Ups (pak), Barbie Sun Set Accessories #1497, Skipper Tea Party #1924, and Skipper Country Picnic #1933.

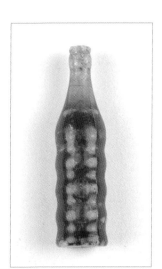

Soda Bottle, $15
Can be found with Barbie Baby Sits #953 and Ken Party Fun (pak).

Box of Pretzels, $15
Can be found with Barbie Baby Sits #953 and Ken Party Fun (pak).

Pink Pot with Black Handle, $65
Can be found with Tutti Cookin' Goodies #3559.

Box of Cookie Mix, $25
Can be found with Skipper Cookie Time #1912.

Silver Tea Kettle, $25
Can be found with Barbie's Hostess Set #1034, Barbie Learns To Cook #1634, and Barbie Lunchtime #1673.

Aqua Placemat with Fringed Ends, $15
Can be found with Barbie's Hostess Set #1034 and Barbie and Midge Set n' Serve (pak).

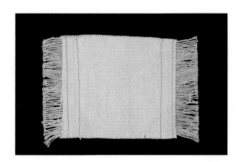

White Placemat with Fringed Ends, $15
Can be found with Skipper Tea Party #1924.

Ceramic Stein with Metal Lid, $35
Can be found with Ken In Switzerland #776.

Silver Monogram "B" Teapot with Lid, $25
Can be found with Barbie's Hostess Set #1034, Barbie Invitation To Tea #1632, Barbie and Midge Set n' Serve (pak), Barbie Cook-Ups (pak), and Skipper Tea Party #1924.

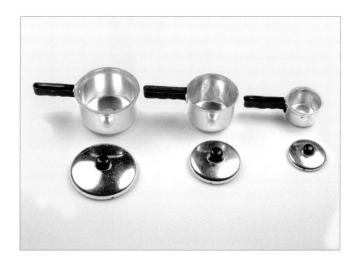

Large Pot with Lid, $25
Can be found with Barbie's Hostess Set #1034, Barbie Learns To Cook #1634, and Barbie Kitchen Magic (pak).

Medium Pot with Lid, $25
Can be found with Barbie's Hostess Set #1034, Barbie Learns To Cook #1634, Barbie Kitchen Magic (pak), and Barbie Lunchtime #1673.

Small Pot with Lid, $25
Can be found with Barbie's Hostess Set #1034, Barbie Learns To Cook #1634, and Barbie Kitchen Magic (pak).

Silver Boiler Pan, $25
Can be found with Barbie Learns To Cook #1634 and Skipper Cookie Time #1912.

Casserole Handle, $40
Can be found with Barbie's Hostess Set #1034, Barbie Brunch Time #1628, Barbie and Midge Set n' Serve (pak), and Barbie Cook-Ups (pak).

Toaster, $15
Can be found with Barbie's Hostess Set #1034, Barbie Learns To Cook #1634, Barbie Kitchen Magic (pak), Barbie Lunchtime #1673, and Barbie Cook-Ups (pak).

Large Casserole Dish with Lid, $25
Can be found with Barbie's Hostess Set #1034, Barbie Brunch Time #1628, Barbie and Midge Set n' Serve (pak), and Barbie Cook-Ups (pak).

Medium Casserole Dish with Lid, $25
Can be found with Barbie's Hostess Set #1034, Barbie Brunch Time #1628, Barbie and Midge Set n' Serve (pak), Coffee's On #1670, and Barbie Cook-Ups (pak).

Small Casserole Dish with Lid, $25
Can be found with Barbie's Hostess Set #1034, Barbie Brunch Time #1628, Barbie and Midge Set n' Serve (pak), and Barbie Cook-Ups (pak).

Metal Candelabra with Pink Painted Candle, $95
Can be found with Barbie's Hostess Set #1034.

Paper Lace Doily, $35
Can be found with Barbie's Hostess Set #1034 and Skipper Happy Birthday #1919.

Coffeemaker with Lid, $25
Can be found with Barbie's Hostess Set #1034, Barbie Brunch Time #1628, Barbie Kitchen Magic (pak), Coffee's On #1670, and Barbie Cook-Ups (pak).

White Plastic Pitcher, $45
Can be found with Barbie Lovely n' Lavender #3358.

White Plastic Tumbler, $65
Can be found with Barbie Lovely n' Lavender #3358.

Thermos with Lid, $35
Can be found with Skipper Country Picnic #1933.

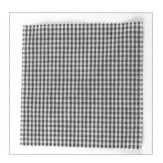

Small Red and White Napkin, $20
Can be found with Skipper Country Picnic #1933.

White Paper Napkin with Pink and Blue Detail, $25
Can be found with Skipper Happy Birthday #1919 and Francie Dance Party #1257.

Yellow Bowl, $35
Can be found with Barbie and Francie Color Magic Fashion Fun #4041 and Barbie Color Magic Doll and Costume Set #1043.

White Paper Napkin, $35
Can be found with Barbie Have Fun (pak) and Ken Fountain Boy #1407.

Color Changer Packet B, $25
Can be found with Barbie and Francie Color Magic Fashion Fun #4041, Barbie and Francie Color Magic Fashion Designer Set #4040, Barbie Color Magic Doll and Costume Set #1043, Barbie Color Magic Stripes Away #1775, Barbie Color Magic Smart Switch #1776, Barbie Color Magic Pretty Wild #1777, and Barbie Color Magic Bloom Bursts #1778.

Color Changer Packet A, $25
Can be found with Barbie and Francie Color Magic Fashion Fun #4041, Barbie and Francie Color Magic Fashion Designer Set #4040, Barbie Color Magic Doll and Costume Set #1043, Barbie Color Magic Stripes Away #1775, Barbie Color Magic Smart Switch #1776, Barbie Color Magic Pretty Wild #1777, and Barbie Color Magic Bloom Bursts #1778.

Yellow Applicator, $35 (missing foam in picture)
Can be found with Barbie and Francie Color Magic Fashion Fun #4041, Barbie and Francie Color Magic Fashion Designer Set #4040, Barbie Color Magic Stripes Away #1775, Barbie Color Magic Smart Switch #1776, Barbie Color Magic Pretty Wild #1777, Barbie Color Magic Bloom Bursts #1778, and Barbie Color Magic Doll and Costume Set #1043.

Red Applicator, $25
Can be found with Barbie and Francie Color Magic Fashion Fun #4041, Barbie and Francie Color Magic Fashion Designer Set #4040, Barbie Color Magic Stripes Away #1775, Barbie Color Magic Smart Switch #1776, Barbie Color Magic Pretty Wild #1777, Barbie Color Magic Bloom Bursts #1778, and Barbie Color Magic Doll and Costume Set #1043.

Red and White Napkin, $25
Can be found with Barbie Little Red Riding Hood and The Wolf #880.

Yellow, Pink, and Green Napkins, $25 each
Can be found with Skipper Let's Play House #1934.

Straw Basket, $25
Can be found with Barbie Little Red Riding Hood and The Wolf #880.

Red and White Picnic Blanket, $25
Can be found with Skipper Country Picnic #1933.

White Stove, $65
Can be found with Tutti
Cookin' Goodies #3559.

Chocolate Sundae, $25
Can be found with Skipper
Posy Party #1955, Skipper
Knit Bit #1969, Tutti and Todd
Sundae Treat #3556, Barbie
Goodies Galore #1511, and
Francie Dance Party #1257.

Strawberry Sundae, $25
Can be found with Tutti and
Todd Sundae Treat #3556.

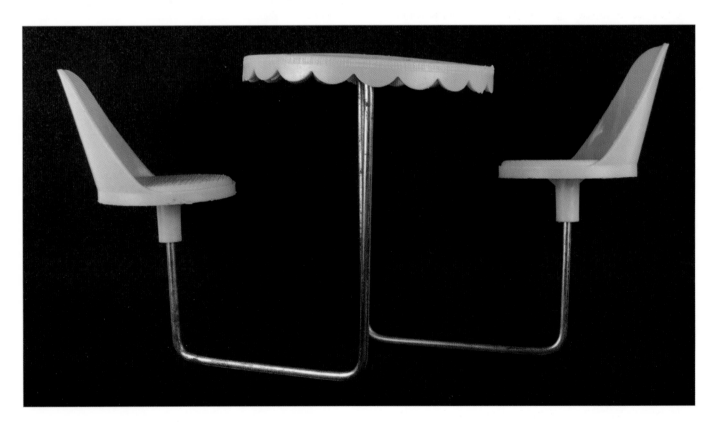

Pink Parlor Table and Chairs, $45
Can be found with Tutti and Todd Sundae Treat #3556.

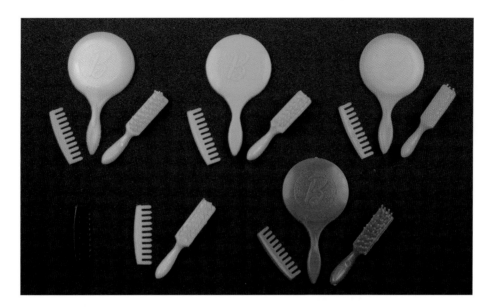

Yellow Comb, $5
Can be found with Francie Nighty Brights (pak) and Skipper Super Snoozers #3371.

Yellow Hand Mirror, $5
Can be found with Skipper Super Snoozers #3371.

Yellow Brush, $5
Can be found Francie Nighty Brights (pak), Skipper Super Snoozers #3371, and Skipper Wooly PJ's (pak).

Aqua Comb, $5
Can be found with Barbie Underprints #1685, Barbie Sun Set Accessories #1497, Francie Nighty Brights (pak), Francie Sleepy Time Gal #3364, Tutti and Todd Sundae Treat #3556, and Tutti Pinky PJ's #3616.

Aqua Hand Mirror, $5
Can be found with Barbie Underprints #1685, Barbie Sun Set Accessories #1497, and Francie Sleepy Time Gal #3364.

Aqua Hair Brush, $5
Can be found with Barbie Underprints #1685, Barbie Sun Set Accessories #1497, Francie Nighty Brights (pak), Francie Sleepy Time Gal #3364, Tutti and Todd Sundae Treat #3556, and Tutti Pinky PJ's #3616.

Pink Comb, $5
Can be found with Barbie Floral Petticoat #921, Barbie Roman Holiday #968, Barbie Boudoir (pak), Barbie Ruffles n' Lace (pak), Barbie Glamour Group #1510, Barbie Fashion Bouquet #1511, Barbie Sweet Dreams #3350, Francie Hair-Dos (pak), Skipper Underpretties #1900, Skipper Beauty Bath (pak), Skipper Baby Dolls #1957, Tutti Walkin' My Dolly #3552, Tutti Night Night, Sleep Tight #3553, Tutti Melody In Pink #3555, and Tutti Cookin' Goodies #3559.

Pink Hand Mirror, $5
Can be found with Barbie Floral Petticoat #921, Barbie Lingerie Pak, Barbie Boudoir (pak), Barbie Ruffles n' Lace (pak), Barbie Sweet Dreams #3350, Francie Tuckered Out #1253, Francie Hair-Dos (pak), Francie Snooze News #3453 (1970), Skipper Underpretties #1900, and Skipper Beauty Bath (pak).

Pink Hair Brush, $5
Can be found with Barbie Floral Petticoat #921, Barbie Boudoir (pak), Barbie Ruffles n' Lace (pak), Barbie Glamour Group #1510, Barbie Fashion Bouquet #1511, Barbie Sweet Dreams #3350, Francie Tuckered Out #1253, Francie Hair-Dos (pak), Skipper Underpretties #1900, Skipper Beauty Bath (pak), Skipper Baby Dolls #1957, Tutti Walkin' My Dolly #3552, Tutti Night Night, Sleep Tight #3553, Tutti Melody In Pink #3555, and Tutti Cookin' Goodies #3559.

Black Comb, $10
Can be found with Ken Morning Workout (pak).

White Comb, $5
Can be found with Barbie Dreamland #1669, Barbie Sleeping Pretty #1636, Francie Snappy Snoozers #1238, Francie Rise & Shine #1194, Tutti Me And My Dog #3554, and Tutti Swing-a-Ling #3560.

White Hair Brush, $10
Can be found with Barbie Dreamland #1669, Barbie Sleeping Pretty #1636, Francie Snappy Snoozers #1238, Francie Rise & Shine #1194, Tutti Me And My Dog #3554, and Tutti Swing-a-Ling #3560.

Hot Pink Comb, $5
Can be found with Barbie Petti-Pinks (pak), Twiggy Twigster #1727, Francie Snooze News #1226, Francie Snappy Snoozers #1238, and Francie Snooze News #3453 (1970).

Hot Pink Hand Mirror, $5
Can be found with Barbie Add-Ons (pak) and Twiggy Twigster #1727.

Hot Pink Hair Brush, $5
Can be found with Barbie Petti-Pinks (pak), Twiggy Twigster #1727, Francie Snooze News #1226, Francie Snappy Snoozers #1238, and Francie Snooze News #3453 (1970).

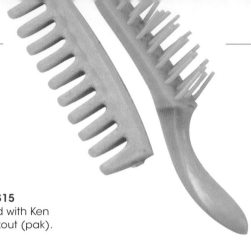

White Soap, $15
Can be found with Ken
Morning Workout (pak).

Blue Sponge, $15
Can be found with Ken
Morning Workout (pak).

Black Comb, $10
Can be found with Ken
Morning Workout (pak).

Blue Comb, $5
Can be found with Barbie
Slumber Party #1642 and
Barbie Sleepytime Gal #1674.

Blue Hair Brush, $5
Can be found with Barbie
Slumber Party #1642 and
Barbie Sleepytime Gal #1674.

Gold Talc Box, $10
Can be found with Barbie
Singing In The Shower #988,
Barbie Boudoir (pak), Barbie
Petti-Pinks (pak), Barbie Perfect
Beginnings (pak), Francie Rise
& Shine #1194, and Skipper
Beauty Bath (pak).

Kleenex Box, $15
Can be found with Barbie Candy
Striper Volunteer #889 and
Skipper Beauty Bath (pak).

Blue Powder Puff, $10
Can be found with Barbie
Singing In The Shower #988,
Barbie Boudoir (pak), Francie
Rise & Shine #1194, and
Skipper Beauty Bath (pak).

White Hankie, $35
Can be found with Barbie
Evening Splendour #961,
Barbie Roman Holiday #968,
Barbie Golden Elegance #992,
and Ken Doctor Kit (pak).

Hot Pink Powder Puff, $15
Can be found with Barbie
Petti-Pinks (pak), Barbie Perfect
Beginnings (pak), and Twiggy
Twigster #1727.

Brass Compact with Powder Puff, $800
Can be found with Barbie Roman Holiday #968.

Blue "Hers" Towel, $8
Can be found with Barbie Singing In The Shower #988 and Barbie Boudoir (pak).

Yellow "His" Towel, $8 per towel
Can be found with Ken Terry Togs #784.

Light Pink Powder Puff, $15
Can be found with Barbie Perfect Beginnings (pak).

Yellow Powder Puff, $25
Can be found with Barbie Perfect Beginnings Color Magic Swimsuit Fabric (pak).

Blue Hand Towel, $10
Can be found with Barbie Singing In The Shower #988 and Barbie Boudoir (pak).

Floral Hand Towel, $15
Can be found with Skipper Beauty Bath (pak).

White Hand Towel, $15
Can be found with Barbie Candy Striper Volunteer #889.

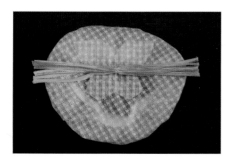

Shower Cap, $10
Can be found with Barbie Singing In The Shower #988, Barbie Bathrobe (pak), Barbie Boudoir (pak), and Skipper Beauty Bath (pak).

Alarm Clock, $8
Can be found with Barbie Sweet Dreams #973, Barbie Baby Sits #953, Ken Sleeper Set #781, Ken Sleeper Set #782, Ken Doctor Kit (pak), Ken Party Fun (pak), and Barbie Pajama Party #1601.

Pink "B" Soap, $15
Can be found with Barbie Singing In The Shower #988.

Sponge with Pink Handle, $10
Can be found with Barbie Singing In The Shower #988, Barbie Boudoir (pak), and Skipper Beauty Bath (pak).

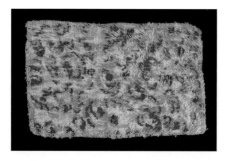

Floral Bath Towel, $15
Can be found with Skipper Beauty Bath (pak).

Hot Pink Fuzzy Scale, $10
Can be found with Barbie Petti-Pinks (pak), Barbie Fashion First (pak), and Francie Get Readies (pak).

Yellow Bath Towel, $8
Can be found with Ken Boxing (pak).

Pink Scale, $15
Can be found with Barbie Slumber Party #1642, Skipper Beauty Bath (pak), and Skipper Baby Dolls #1957.

Pink Razor, $25
Can be found with Barbie Boudoir (pak).

Gray Razor, $15
Can be found with Ken Terry Togs #784, Barbie Boudoir (pak), Ken Morning Workout (pak), Ken Time to Turn In #1418, Ken Breakfast At 7 #1428, and Ken Wide Awake Stripes #3377.

Pink Curler, $5
Can be found with Barbie Slumber Party #1642, Barbie Glamour Group #1510, Barbie Fashion Bouquet #1511, Francie Tuckered Out #1253, Francie Hair-Dos (pak), Skipper Underpretties #1900, Skipper Jamas n' Jaunties #1944, and Skipper Beauty Bath (pak).

Yellow Curler, $10
Can be found with Skipper Super Snoozers #3371.

Brown Eyebrow Pencil, $25
Can be found with Barbie Add-Ons (pak), Barbie Finishing Touch (pak), Barbie Goodies Galore #1511, and Twiggy Twigster #1727.

Bobby "Barbie" Pins, $3 each
Can be found with Barbie Slumber Party #1642, and Francie Rise & Shine #1194.

Hot Pink Cosmetic Case, $15
Can be found with Barbie Add-Ons (pak).

Orange Cosmetic Case, $20
Can be found with Barbie Sun Set Accessories #1497 and Twiggy Twigster #1727.

Brunette Portrait Mirror, $25
Can be found with Barbie Petti-Pinks (pak), Barbie Goodies Galore #1511, Francie Rise & Shine #1194.

Redhead Portrait Mirror, $25
Can be found with Francie Snooze News #1226.

Blonde Portrait Mirror, $25
Can be found with Skipper Eeny Meeny #1974 and Skipper Nighty Nice (pak).

Yellow Sleep Mask, $15
Can be found with Francie Slumber Number #1271.

Black Eyelash Brush, $15
Can be found with Barbie Add-Ons (pak), Barbie Finishing Touches (pak), Barbie Goodies Galore #1511, Barbie Sun Set Accessories #1497, and Twiggy Twigster #1727.

Pink Eyelash Brush, $15
Can be found with Francie Original Outfit.

White Eyelash Brush, $15
Can be found with Francie Original Outfit.

Woven Picnic Basket, $20
Can be found with Barbie
Picnic Set #967.

Scissors, $15
Can be found with Barbie Sweater
Girl #976, Barbie Knitting Pretty
(blue) #957, and Barbie Knitting
Pretty (pink) #957.

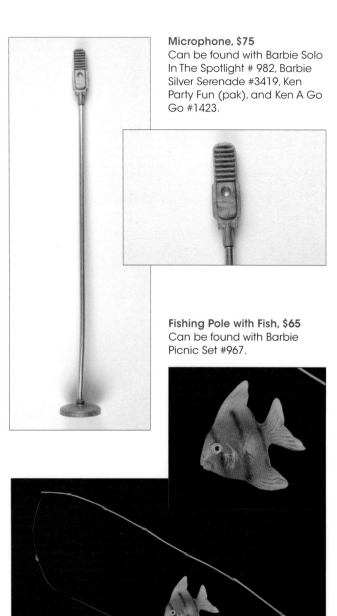

Microphone, $75
Can be found with Barbie Solo
In The Spotlight # 982, Barbie
Silver Serenade #3419, Ken
Party Fun (pak), and Ken A Go
Go #1423.

**Pink, Yellow, and
Green Bowl of
Yarn with Needles,
$15**
Can be found with
Barbie Knitting
Pretty (pink) #957
and Skipper School
Days #1907.

**Red, Yellow, and Green Bowl
of Yarn with Needles, $15**
Can be found with Barbie
Sweater Girl #976, Barbie
Knitting Pretty #957, and
Barbie Leisure Hours (pak).

Fishing Pole with Fish, $65
Can be found with Barbie
Picnic Set #967.

Ukulele, $15
Can be found with Ken Party
Fun (pak) and Ken In Hawaii
#1404.

Artist Portfolio, $25
Can be found with Barbie Busy Gal #981.

"State" School Pennant, $10
Can be found with Ken Campus Hero #770.

Keys on a "K" Key Chain, $35
Can be found with Ken Rally Day and Ken Party Fun (pak).

Artist Sketches, $45
Can be found with Barbie Busy Gal #981.

Tennis Racquet, $8
Can be found with Barbie Tennis Anyone? #941, Ken Time for Tennis #790, Barbie For The Rink and Court (pak), Ken Sportsman (pak), Barbie Goodies Galore #1518, Barbie Tennis Team #1781, Francie Sportin' Set #1044, and Francie Tennis Tunic #1221.

Tennis Ball, $5
Can be found with Barbie Tennis Anyone? #941, Ken Time for Tennis #790, Ken Play Ball #792, Barbie For The Rink and Court (pak), Ken Sportsman (pak), Barbie Goodies Galore #1518, Barbie Tennis Team #1781, Francie Sportin' Set #1044, Francie Tennis Tunic #1221, Skipper Can You Play? #1923, Skipper Tennis Time #3466, Skipper Just For Fun (pak), Ricky Little Leaguer #1504, and Skipper Action Fashion (pak).

Guitar with Black String Strap, $65
Can be found with Ken A Go Go #1423.

Black Plastic Barbell, $5
Can be found with Ken In Training #780, Ken Morning Workout (pak), Barbie Shape-Ups #1782, and Ken Beach Beat #3384.

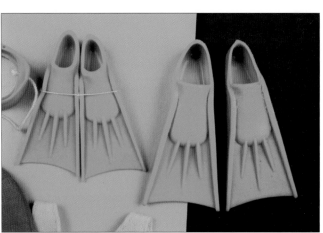

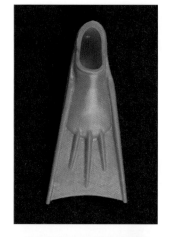

Orange Swim Fins, $10
Can be found with Barbie Scuba Do's #1788 and Barbie Sun Set Accessories #1497.

Orange face Mask, $10
Can be found with Barbie Scuba Do's #1788 and Barbie Sun Set Accessories #1497.

Green Swim Fins for Barbie, $15
Can be found with Barbie Skin Diver #1608.

Green Swim Fins for Ken, $15
Can be found with Ken Snorkel Gear (pak), Ken Skin Diver #1406, and Ken Shoes for Sports (pak).

Orange Snorkel, $10
Can be found with Barbie Scuba Do's #1788 and Barbie Sun Set Accessories #1497.

Green Snorkel, $8
Can be found with Ken Snorkel Gear (pak), Barbie Skin Diver #1608, and Ken Skin Diver #1406.

Green Face Mask, $8
Can be found with Ken Snorkel Gear (pak), Barbie Skin Diver #1608, and Ken Skin Diver #1406.

Aqua Swim Fins, $15
Can be found with Barbie Action Accents #1585.

Aqua Snorkel, $20
Can be found with Barbie Action Accents #1585.

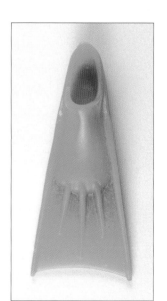

Aqua Face Mask, $15
Can be found with Barbie Action Accents #1585.

Yellow Face Mask, $10
Can be found with Ken
Shore Lines #1435.

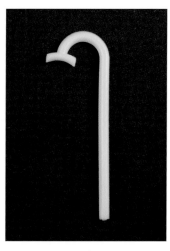

Yellow Snorkel, $10
Can be found with Ken Shore
Lines #1435.

Blue Face Mask, $10
Can be found with Ken
Surf's Up #1248.

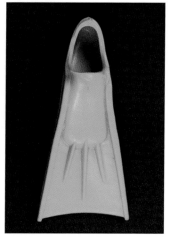

Blue Swim Fins, $10
Can be found with Ken Surf's
Up #1248 and Ken Beach Beat
#3384.

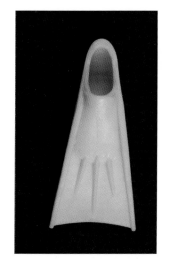

Yellow Swim Fins, $10
Can be found with Ken Shore
Lines #1435, Ken Shoe Ins
(pak).

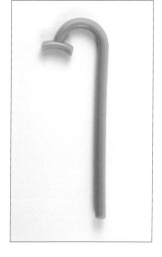

Blue Snorkel, $10
Can be found with Ken Surf's
Up #1248 and Ken Beach Beat
#3384.

Boxing Glove, $8
Can be found with Ken
Boxing (pak) and Ken
Sportsman (pak).

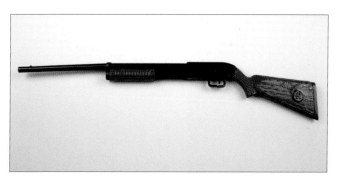

Rifle, $20
Can be found with Hunting Shirt (pak), Ken Going Hunting
#1409, and Ken Sportsman (pak).

Baseball Mitt, $10
Can be found with Ken Play Ball #792, Ken Sportsman (pak), and Ricky Little Leaguer #1504.

Baseball Bat, $15
Can be found with Ken Play Ball #792, Ken Sportsman (pak), and Skipper Just For Fun (pak).

Football, $10
Can be found with Ken Touchdown #799 and Ken Sportsman (pak).

Shoulder Pads, $10
Can be found with Ken Touchdown #799 and Ken Sportsman (pak).

Baton, $20
Can be found with Barbie Drum Majorette #875.

Baton with Gold Cord, $15
Can be found with Ken Drum Major #775.

Croquet Mallet, $15
Can be found with Barb
n' Games #1619 and Ski
Fun Time #1920.

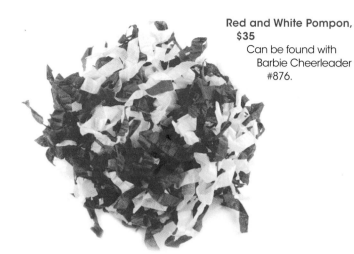

**Red and White Pompon,
$35**
Can be found with
Barbie Cheerleader
#876.

Croquet Ball, $15
Can be found with Barbie Fun
n' Games #1619 and Skipper
Fun Time #1920.

Plastic Megaphone, $15
Can be found with Barbie
Cheerleader #876.

Croquet Metal Wicket, $20
Can be found with Barbie Fun
n' Games #1619 and Skipper
Fun Time #1920.

Croquet Wooden Stake, $20
Can be found with Barbie Fun
n' Games #1619 and Skipper
Fun Time #1920.

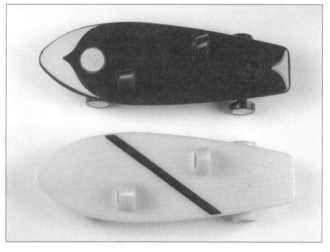

Red Skateboard with Yellow Trim, $35
Can be found with Skipper On Wheels #1032.

Tan Skateboard with Red Stripe, $45
Can be found with Ricky Skateboard Set #1505.

Painting, $95
Can be found with
Barbie Modern Art
#1625.

**Black Elastic Exercise
Cord, $15**
Can be found with Barbie
Action Accents #1585 and
Barbie Shape-Ups #1782.

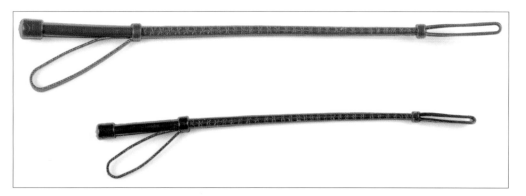

Brown Riding Crop, $65
Can be found with Barbie
Riding In The Park #1668.

Black Riding Crop, $45
Can be found with Skipper
Learning To Ride #1935.

**Twist Board with "Mattel
Twist," $20**
Can be found with Barbie
Shape-Ups #1782.

**Yellow Boogie
Board with
Flowers, $35**
Can be found
with Barbie Sun
Set Accessories
#1497.

**Red Boogie
Board with Blue
Stripe, $25**
Can be found
with Ken Beach
Beat #3384.

Twist Board with Stripes, $20
Can be found with Barbie
Shape-Ups #1782.

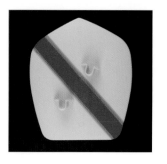

**Yellow Boogie Board with Red
Stripe, $45**
Can be found with Ken Surf's
Up #1248.

Yellow Teeter Board, $35
Can be found with Skipper
Teeter Timers #3467.

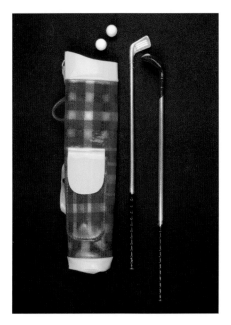

Golf Bag, $20
Can be found
with Barbie
Golfing Greats
#3413 and Ken
Golf Gear (pak).

**Golf Clubs (wood
& putter), $35**
Can be found
with Barbie
Golfing Greats
#3413 and Ken
Golf Gear (pak).

Golf Ball, $20
Can be found with Barbie
Golfing Greats #3413 and
Ken Golf Gear (pak).

Red Scooter, $65
Can be found with
Skipper On Wheels
#1032.

**Yellow Guitar with Brown
Strap, $25**
Can be found with Live
Action P.J. On Stage #1153.

Telephones

Pink Telephone with Metal Dial, $35
Can be found with Barbie Suburban Shopper #969.

White Telephone, $15
Can be found with Sheath Skirt and Telephone (pak), Barbie Baby Sits #953, and Barbie Busy Morning #956.

Pink Telephone, $25
Can be found with Barbie Suburban Shopper #969.

Black Telephone, $15
Can be found with Sheath Skirt and Telephone (pak).

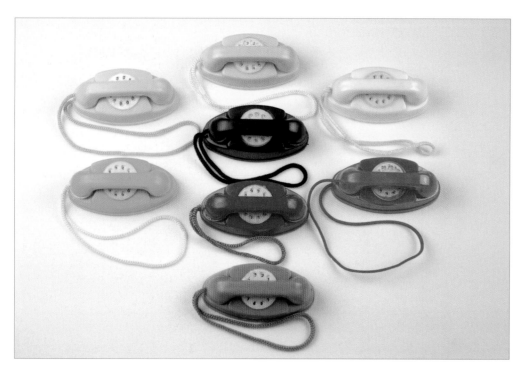

Pink Princess Telephone, $20
Can be found with Skipper School's Cool #1976.

Black Princess Telephone, $10
Can be found with Ken Party Fun (pak).

Red Princess Telephone, $10
Can be found with Ken Morning Workout (pak) and Barbie Goodies Galore #1518.

Tan Princess Telephone, $10
Can be found with Barbie Leisure Hours (pak).

White Princess Telephone, $15
Can be found with Barbie Boudoir (pak) and Ken Doctor Kit (pak).

Hot Pink Princess Telephone, $35
Can be found with Skipper School's Cool #1976.

Light Blue Princess Telephone, $10
Can be found with Skipper Dreamtime #1909.

Aqua Princess Telephone, $10
Can be found with Skipper Nighty Nice (pak).

Black Headband Bow, $175
Can be found with Barbie Easter Parade #971.

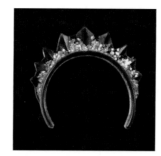

Clear Molded Tiara with Glitter Applied, $75
Can be found with Francie Miss Teenage Beauty #1284.

Silver Paper Tiara, $25
Can be found with Barbie Ballerina #989.

White Hair Bow with Embroidered Flower, $65
Can be found with Francie Cool White #1280.

Gray Plastic Tiara, $45
Can be found with Barbie Sophisticated Lady #993.

Clear Molded Tiara with Glitter in The Plastic, $45
Can be found with Barbie Sophisticated Lady #993.

Blonde Braid Headband with Pink Ribbons, $20
Can be found with Francie Summer Frost #1276 and Francie Hair Dos (pak).

Brunette Braid Headband with Pink Ribbons, $20
Can be found with Francie Summer Frost #1276 and Francie Hair Dos (pak).

Blonde Braid with Red Bow, $20
Can be found with Barbie Fancy Trimmings (pak), Barbie Add-Ons (pak), Barbie All The Trimmings (pak), Francie Summer Coolers #1292, and Francie Hair Dos (pak).

Brunette Braid with Red Bow, $20
Can be found with Barbie Fancy Trimmings (pak), Barbie Add-Ons (pak), Barbie All The Trimmings (pak), Francie Summer Coolers #1292, and Francie Hair Dos (pak).

Silver Foil Crown, $75
Can be found with Francie Twilight Twinkle #3459.

Light Pink Braid with Green Ribbon, $45
Can be found with Francie Pazam! #1213.

Hot Pink Braid with Green Ribbon, $45
Can be found with Francie Pazam! #1213.

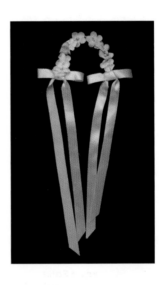

Floral Headband with Pink Ribbon, $25
Can be found with Skipper Ballet Class #1905.

Headband with Gold Braid, $65
Can be found with Francie Prom Pinks #1295.

Gold Stretch Headband, $15
Can be found with Skipper Silk n' Fancy #1902.

Headband with Black Velvet, $65
Can be found with Francie Two For The Ball #1232.

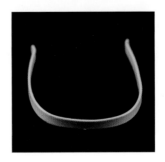

Yellow Metal Headband, $65
Can be found with Skipper Beachy Peachy #1938.

Yellow Floral Headband, $20
Can be found with Skipper Flower Girl #1904.

Pink Flower Buds, $35
Can be found with Barbie In Japan #821.

Blue Satin Hair Ribbon, $45
Can be found with Skipper Happy Birthday #1919.

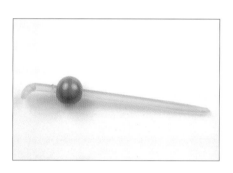

Plastic Stick with Orange, $45
Can be found with Barbie In Japan #821.

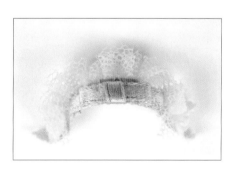

Aqua Satin Headband with Yellow Tulle, $35
Can be found with Tutti Flower Girl #3615.

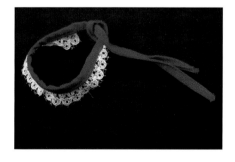

Red Cotton Headband with Lace, $25
Can be found with Tutti Let's Play Barbie #3608.

Multicolored Flower with Silver Dangles, $45
Can be found with Barbie In Japan #821.

Pink Stuffed Dog, $15
Can be found with Barbie Nighty Negligee #965.

Blue Stuffed Cat, $15
Can be found with Skipper Dreamtime #1909.

Pink Record Player, $25
Can be found with Francie Go Granny Go #1267 and Francie Sugar Sheers #1229.

Clown Doll, $25
Can be found with Tutti Clowning Around #3606.

Blue Barbie Record Player, $15
Can be found with Barbie Hostess Set #1034, Barbie Dancing Doll #1626, Barbie Disc Date #1633, Have Fun (pak), Barbie Sun Set Accessories #1497, Francie Dance Party #1257, Francie Go Granny Go #1267, and Francie Sugar Sheers #1229.

Pink Record Player with White Needle Arm, $30
Can be found with Barbie Sun Set Accessories #1497 and Skipper Happy Times (pak).

Masquerade Face Mask, $15
Can be found with Ken Masquerade #794.

Masquerade Mask, $15
Can be found with Barbie Masquerade #944, Skipper Masquerade #1903, and Barbie Dog n' Duds #1613.

Red Barbie Record, $10
Can be found with Barbie Hostess Set #1034, Barbie Dancing Doll #1626, Barbie Disc Date #1633, Have Fun (pak), Barbie Sun Set Accessories #1497, Francie Dance Party #1257, Francie Go Granny Go #1267, Francie Sugar Sheers #1229, and Skipper Happy Times (pak).

Blue Barbie Record, $10
Can be found with Barbie Hostess Set #1034, Barbie Dancing Doll #1626, Barbie Disc Date #1633, Have Fun (pak), Barbie Sun Set Accessories #1497, Francie Dance Party #1257, Francie Go Granny Go #1267, and Francie Sugar Sheers #1229.

Francie Record Sleeve, $25
Can be found with Francie Go Granny Go #1267.

Blue and Yellow Ball, $65
Can be found with Jamie Strollin' In Style #1247.

Tan Television, $15
Can be found with Barbie Leisure Hours (pak), Have Fun (pak), and Ken T.V.'s Good Tonight #1419.

Green and Yellow Ball, $45
Can be found with Skipper Young Ideas #1513 and Tutti Sea Shore Shorties #3614.

Brown Television, $20
Can be found with Ken Party Fun (pak) and Barbie Sun Set Accessories #1497.

Orange and Blue Ball, $45
Can be found with Barbie Sun Set Accessories #1497 and Skipper Jeepers Creepers #1966.

Camera, $25
Can be found with Barbie Vacation Time #1623, Barbie Aboard Ship #1631, Barbie Fashion Editor #1635, Barbie Photo Fashion #1648, Ken Rovin' Reporter #1417, Barbie International Fair #1653, Barbie Club Meeting #1672, Barbie See-Worthy #1872, Barbie Tour-Ins (pak), Twiggy Gear #1728, Francie The Wild Bunch #1766, Skipper Ship Ahoy #1918, and Ken Sun Fun (pak).

Yellow, Blue, Pink, and Green Rubber Ball, $35
Can be found with Skipper Country Picnic #1933.

Light Blue Satin Pillow, $35
Can be found with Barbie
Sleeping Pretty #1636.

Blue Sailboat, $35
Can be found with
Barbie Sun Set
Accessories #1497
and Tutti Sea Shore
Shorties #3614.

Red Sailboat, $35
Can be found with
Skipper Ship Ahoy
#1918.

Mini Barbie Doll, $45
Can be found with Skipper Day
At The Fair #1911, Skipper Me
n' My Doll #1913, and Skipper
Just For Fun (pak).

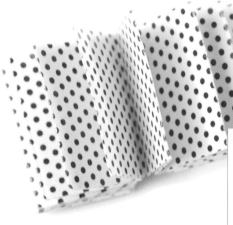

White Cards with Red Dots Set of 26, $65
Can be found with Francie The Bridge
Bit #1279.

**Mini Barbie Doll Red Gingham
Skirt, $25**
Can be found with Skipper Just
For Fun (pak).

**Mini Barbie Doll Pink Gingham
Skirt, $35**
Can be found with Skipper
Me n' My Doll #1913.

Pink Pillow with Flower Print, $35
Can be found with Francie The Bridge Bit #1279.

Red Yo-Yo, $15
Can be found with Skipper On Wheels #1032, Skipper Outdoor Casuals #1915, and Skipper Just For Fun (pak).

Royal Blue Transistor Radio, $35
Can be found with Francie Zig-Zag Zoom #3445.

Gold Wrapped Present with Red, $30
Can be found with Skipper Happy Birthday #1919.

Yellow Transistor Radio, $35
Can be found with Francie Zig-Zag Zoom #3445 and Skipper Action Fashion (pak).

Gold Wrapped Present with No Tag, $20
Can be found with Skipper Young Ideas #1513 and Tutti Birthday Beauties #3617.

Hot Pink Wrapped Present, $25
Can be found with Skipper Eeny Meeny #1974.

Pink Popper Party Favor with Glitter, $20
Can be found with Skipper Happy Birthday #1919 and Tutti Birthday Beauties #3617.

Pink Candle, $15
Can be found with Skipper
Happy Birthday #1919.

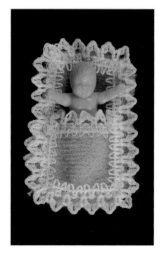

Baby In Bunting, $25
Can be found with Tutti Pinky
PJ's #3616.

**Jump Rope with Black
Handle, $15**
Can be found with Skipper
Skippin' Rope #3604 and
Skipper Just For Fun (pak).

**Jump Rope with Red Handle,
$15**
Can be found with Skipper
Can You Play? #1923.

**Baby in Pink and Blue Cradle,
$45**
Can be found with Skipper
Let's Play House #1932.

**Jump Rope with Clear
Handle, $15**
Can be found with Skipper
Knit Bit #1969, Skipper Young
Ideas #1513, Skipper Happy
Times (pak), and Skipper
Action Fashion (pak).

**Checkerboard
with Checkers,
$65**
Can be found with
Skipper Rainy Day
Checkers #1928.

Butterfly Net with Paper Butterfly, $45
Can be found with Skipper Country Picnic #1933.

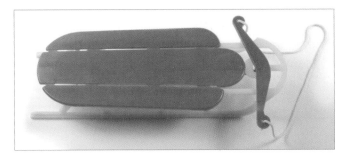

Hot Pink Sled, $65
Can be found with Skipper Goin' Sleddin' #3475.

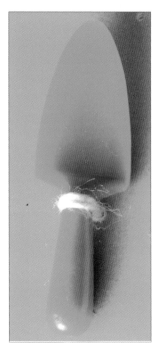

Green Trowel, $25
Can be found with Plantin' Posies #3609.

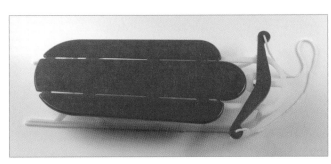

Red Sled, $75
Can be found with Skipper Sledding Fun #1936.

Green Watering Can with Lid, $45
Can be found with Plantin' Posies #3609.

Red Sand Pail, $25
Can be found with Tutti Sand Castles #3603.

Dear Diary, $10
Can be found with Barbie Sweet Dreams #973.

"How To Knit," $10
Can be found with Barbie Sweater Girl #976, Barbie Knitting Pretty (blue) #957, and Barbie Knitting Pretty (pink) #957.

How To Design Your Own Fashion, $35
Can be found with Barbie Junior Designer #1620.

How To Sail A Boat, $15
Can be found with Ken The Yachtsman #789.

Mattel Daily Newspaper, $45
Can be found with Barbie Knit Hit #1621 and Ken Business Appointment #1424.

Seed Packet, $45
Can be found with Plantin' Posies #3609

Nursery Rhymes Book, $45
Can be found with Skipper Let's Play House #1932.

Tennis Rules, $15
Can be found with Barbie Tennis Anyone? #941.

Road Map, $15
Can be found with Barbie Open Road #985, Ken Rally Day #788, Ken Doctor Kit (pak), and Ken Party Fun (pak).

Telephone Numbers For Baby Sitter, $15
Can be found with Barbie Baby Sits #953.

How To Travel Book, $10
Can be found with Barbie Baby Sits #953 and Barbie Aboard Ship #1631.

How to Get A Raise Book, $10
Can be found with Barbie Baby Sits #953 and Ken Off To Bed #1413.

How To Lose Weight Book, $10
Can be found with Barbie Baby Sits #953, Barbie Slumber Party #1642, and Barbie Sleepytime Gal #1674.

A Tale Of Two Cities Book, $25
Can be found with Ken Off To Bed #1413.

Mattel Art Gallery Program, $125
Can be found with Barbie Modern Art #1625.

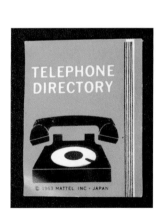

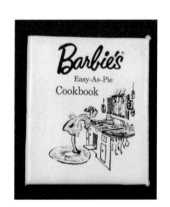

Barbie's Easy-As-Pie Cookbook, $25
Can be found with Barbie Learns To Cook #1634 and Skipper Cookie Time #1912.

Blue Telephone Directory, $15
Can be found with Ken Doctor Kit (pak) and Ken Party Fun (pak).

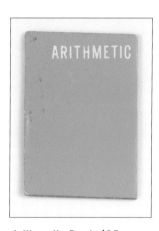

Arithmetic Book, $15
Can be found with Skipper School Girl #1921, Skipper Hearts n' Flowers #1945, Skipper Skimmy Stripes #1956, and Skipper Happy Times (pak).

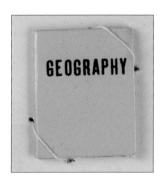

English Book, $15
Can be found with Skipper School Girl #1921, Skipper Hearts n' Flowers #1945, Skipper Skimmy Stripes #1956, and Skipper Happy Times (pak).

Geography Book, $20
Can be found with Barbie Student Teacher #1622 and Skipper School Girl #1921.

"How To Build Muscles" Book, $8
Can be found with Ken Morning Workout (pak).

Travel Poster, $125
Can be found with Barbie Aboard Ship #1631.

"Come To My Party" Invitation, $15
Can be found with Barbie Masquerade #944, Ken Party Fun (pak), and Skipper Masquerade #1903.

Ballet Poster for Barbie, $15
Can be found with Barbie Ballerina #989.

Nutcracker Suite Paper Program, $20
Can be found with Skipper Ballet Class #1905.

BALLET COMPANY
Presents
NUTCRACKER SUITE

Clara...Skipper T.M.
Music...Tchaikowsky

Mexico Map, $25
Can be found with Barbie Aboard Ship #1631 and Skipper Ship Ahoy #1918.

Hawaii Map, $25
Can be found with Barbie Aboard Ship #1631 and Skipper Ship Ahoy #1918.

Niagara Falls Map, $35
Can be found with Barbie Aboard Ship #1631.

Flight Log (Made in Japan), $45
Can be found with Ken American Airlines Captain #779.

Living Barbie Exercise Book, $15
Can be found with Barbie Shape-Ups #1782.

Barbie's Baby Sitter's Manual Book, $35
Can be found with Barbie Baby Sits #953 1965 version.

Formula Recipe, $45
Can be found with Barbie Baby Sits #953 1965 version.

"I'm Having A Party" Invitation, $15
Can be found with Skipper Happy Birthday #1919, Skipper Young Ideas #1513, and Tutti Birthday Beauties #3617.

Army and Air Force Card, $25
Can be found with Ken Army and Air Force #797.

How To Play Bridge Book, $45
Can be found with Francie The Bridge Bit #1279.

Rolled Up Diploma Tied with a White Bow, $15
Can be found with Barbie Graduation #945 and Ken Graduation #795.

Red Telephone Directory, $15
Can be found with Skipper Dreamtime #1909.

Fuchsia Skis, $35
Can be found with Barbie Action Accents #1585.

Fuchsia Ski Poles, $35
Can be found with Barbie Action Accents #1585.

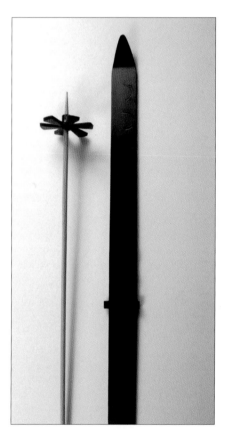

Brown Skis, $15
Can be found with Barbie Ski Queen #948 and Ken Ski Champion #798.

Brown Ski Poles, $15
Can be found with Barbie Ski Queen #948 and Ken Ski Champion #798.

Yellow Skis, $25
Can be found with Ken The Skiing Scene #1438.

Blue Ski Poles, $25
Can be found with Ken The Skiing Scene #1438.

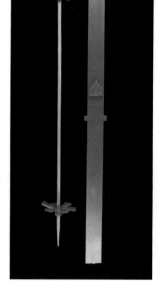

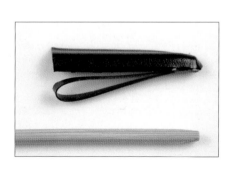

Orange Skis, $25
Can be found with Barbie The Ski Scene #1797.

Orange Ski Poles, $25
Can be found with Barbie The Ski Scene #1797.

Hot Water Bottle, $10
Can be found with Barbie Registered Nurse #991 and Ken Doctor Kit (pak).

Bassinet with Liner, $10
Can be found with Barbie Baby Sits #953.

Medicine Bottle, $15
Can be found with Barbie Registered Nurse #991 and Ken Doctor Kit (pak).

Baby Bottle, $15
Can be found with Barbie Baby Sits #953.

Baby, $20
Can be found with Barbie Baby Sits #953.

Pink Pillow, $15
Can be found with Barbie Baby Sits #953.

Textured Book Strap, $10
Can be found with Barbie Baby Sits #953.

Blue and White Baby Blanket, $15
Can be found with Barbie Baby Sits #953.

Cloth Diaper with Safety Pin, $15
Can be found with Barbie Baby Sits #953.

Baby Robe, $15
Can be found with Barbie Baby Sits #953.

Shiny Book Strap, $20
Can be found with Skipper School Girl #1921, Skipper Hearts n' Flowers #1945, Skipper Skimmy Stripes #1956, and Skipper Happy Times (pak).

Stethoscope, $20
Can be found with Ken Dr. Ken #793 and Ken Doctor Kit (pak).

Head Mirror, $15
Can be found with Ken Dr. Ken #793 and Ken Doctor Kit (pak).

MD Doctors Bag, $15
Can be found with Ken Dr. Ken #793 and Ken Doctor Kit (pak).

Typewriter, $45
Can be found with Ken College Student #1416.

Iron, $25
Can be found with Barbie Junior Designer #1620.

Globe, $45
Can be found with Barbie Student Teacher #1622.

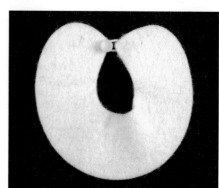

Floral Appliqués, $75
Can be found with Barbie Junior Designer #1620.

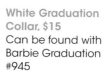

White Graduation Collar, $15
Can be found with Barbie Graduation #945

Order Pad, $35
Can be found with Ken
Fountain Boy #1407.

Tan Pencil, $15
Can be found with Skipper
School Girl #1921, Skipper
Hearts n' Flowers #1945, Skipper
Skimmy Stripes #1956, and
Skipper Happy Times (pak).

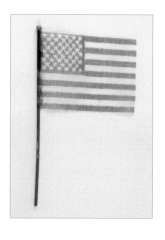

American Flag, $65
Can be found with Barbie Miss
Astronaut #1641 and Ken Mr.
Astronaut #1415.

**Black Briefcase,
$95**
Can be found
with Ken Business
Appointment
#1424.

Red Pencil, $15
Can be found with Skipper
School Girl #1921, Skipper
Hearts n' Flowers #1945, Skipper
Skimmy Stripes #1956, and
Skipper Happy Times (pak).

Brown Pencil, $15
Can be found with Ken Fountain
Boy #1407.

Pointer, $45
Can be found with Barbie
Student Teacher #1622.

Nurse Diploma, $25
Can be found with
Barbie Registered
Nurse #991.

Gold Metal Trophy, $125
Can be found with Barbie
Poodle Parade #1643.

**Metal "B" Loving
Cup Trophy, $145**
Can be found with
Barbie Campus
Sweetheart #1616.

**First Prize
Certificate, $65**
Can be found
with Barbie
Poodle Parade
#1643.

**Metal "F" Loving Cup Trophy,
$145**
Can be found with Francie
Miss Teenage Beauty #1284.

**Miss Teenage Beauty Sash,
$165**
Can be found with Francie
Miss Teenage Beauty #1284.

Pink Chiffon Scarf, $20
Can be found with Barbie Solo In The Spotlight #982 and Barbie Square Neck Sweater (pak).

Black Lace Mantilla, $35
Can be found with Barbie In Mexico #820.

Gold Knit Scarf, $15
Can be found with Ken Fun On Ice #791.

Pink Feather Boa, $65
Can be found with Barbie Pink Formal #1681.

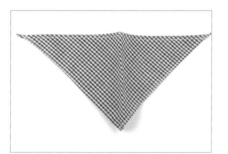

Red and White Neckerchief, $35
Can be found with Ken Cheerful Chef (pak).

Aqua Scarf, $75
Can be found with Barbie London Tour #1661.

Red Pattern Neck Scarf, $25
Can be found with Ken In Holland #0777.

Yellow Scarf, $65
Can be found with Barbie Sun
Set Accessories #1497.

Royal Blue Scarf, $65
Can be found with Barbie Sun
Set Accessories #1497.

Green Scarf, $65
Can be found with Barbie Sun
Set Accessories #1497.

Royal Blue
Neckerchief with
Silver Tie, $35
Can be found with
Barbie Now Knit
#1452.

Yellow Sheer
Scarf with Flower,
$45
Can be found with
Francie Check This
#1291.

Visor with Yellow Scarf, $25
Can be found with Barbie Shoe
Bag #1498 and Barbie Goodies
Galore #1518.

Orange and Yellow Knit
Scarf, $35
Can be found with Twiggy
Twigster #1727.

Orange Visor with
Blue Scarf and
Cinch Ring, $65
Can be found
with Skipper
Jeepers Creepers
#1966.

Purple Scarf, $45
Can be found with Barbie
Silver Blues #3357.

Orange Knit Scarf, $15
Can be found with
Barbie Shift Into Knit
#1478.

Red Knit Scarf, $15
Can be found with Barbie
Super Scarf #3408.

Aqua Plush Boa, $75
Can be found with
Barbie Silver Serenade
#3419.

Hot Pink Knit Scarf, $45
Can be found with Francie
The Combo #1215.

**Red, White, and Blue
Scarf, $25**
Can be found with
Skipper Long n' Short Of
It #3478.

**Red, White, and Purple
Scarf, $25**
Can be found with
Skipper Long n' Short Of
It #3478.

Red Nylon Neckerchief, $20
Can be found with Ken Way
Out West #1720.

White Scarf with Fringe, $45
Can be found with Francie
Long On Leather #1769.

Red Nylon Scarf, $15
Can be found with Francie Midi Plaid #3444.

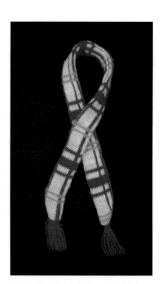

Orange Plaid Scarf, $20
Can be found with Barbie
Anti-Freezers #1464

Green Scarf, $45
Can be found with Francie Plaid
Plans #1767.

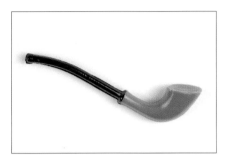

Brown Plastic Pipe, $35
Can be found with Ken In Switzerland #776.

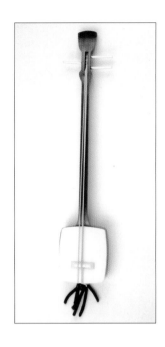

Samisen, $65
Can be found with Barbie In Japan #821.

Gold and Black Fan, $35
Can be found with Barbie In Japan #821.

Ankle Flower Lei, $75
Can be found with Barbie In Hawaii #1605

Tan Lei, $35
Can be found with Ken In Hawaii #1404.

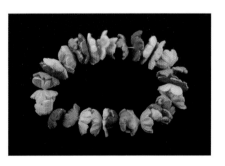

Flower Lei, $25
Can be found with Barbie In Hawaii #1605.

Straw Basket with Handle, $25
Can be found with Barbie
Little Red Riding Hood and the
Wolf #880.

Wolf Mask Wearing Tie, $35
Can be found with Barbie
Little Red Riding Hood and the
Wolf #880.

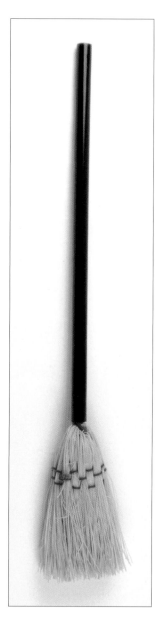

Broom, $20
Can be found with Cinderella
#872 and Leisure Hours (pak).

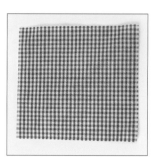

**Large Red and White Check
Napkin, $25**
Can be found with Barbie
Little Red Riding Hood and the
Wolf #880.

Velvet Pillow, $45
Can be found with Ken The
Prince #772.

Red Armlet, $15
Can be found with Barbie
Guinevere #873.

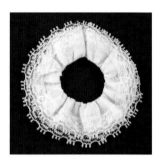

White Neck Ruff, $25
Can be found with Ken The
Prince #772.

Gold Lamp, $25
Can be found with Barbie
Arabian Nights #874.

Scabbard, $25
Can be found with Ken King
Arthur #773.

Sword, $25
Can be found with Ken King
Arthur #773.

Red Spur, $25
Can be found with Ken King
Arthur #773.

Paper Shield, $35
Can be found with Ken King
Arthur #773.

Black Rimmed Cat Eye Glasses, $20
Can be found with Barbie Busy Gal #981, Barbie Registered Nurse #991, Barbie Doll Accessories #923, and Barbie Baby Sits #953.

Red Rimmed Cat Eye Glasses, $85
Can be found with Barbie Open Road #985.

Black Rimmed Cat Eye Glasses in Case (case only), $175.
Can be found with Barbie Roman Holiday #968.

White Rimmed Cat Eye Glasses with Red and Gold Glitter, $25
Can be found with Barbie Accessory Pak and Barbie Knit Skirt (pak).

Brown Rimmed Cat Eye Glasses, $85
Can be found with Barbie Poodle Parade #1643.

White Rimmed Cat Eye Glasses, $25
Can be found with Barbie Helenca Swimsuit (pak), Barbie Knit Top (pak), and In The Swim (pak).

Brown Rimmed Glasses, $45
Can be found with Skipper School Girl #1921.

Blue Sunglasses Goggles, $20
Can be found with Barbie Tennis Anyone? #941, Barbie Ski Queen #948, and Barbie For Rink and Court (pak).

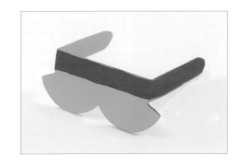

Green Sunglasses with Pink Band, $125
Can be found with Francie Pink Lightning #1231.

Green Sunglasses Goggles, $25
Can be found with Ken Time For Tennis #790, Ken Ski Champion #798, Ken Beach Beat #3384, and Ken Sun Fun (pak).

Green Sunglasses with Pink Dots, $125
Can be found with Francie Culotte-Wot #1214.

Red Sunglasses, $65
Can be found with Skipper On Wheels #1032 and Skipper Land and Sea #1917.

Orange Ski Mask Goggles, $20
Can be found with Barbie The Ski Scene #1797.

Green Sunglasses with Pink Stripes, $75
Can be found with Barbie Trailblazers #1846.

Black Granny Glasses, $45
Can be found with Francie Summer Coolers #1292, Skipper All Spruced Up #1941, Skipper Hearts n' Flowers #1945, and Buffy and Mrs. Beasley.

Blue Plastic Sunglasses with Green Stripe, $35
Can be found with Francie Gad-Abouts #1250.

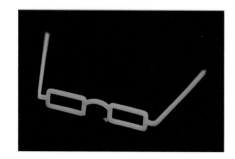

Lime Green Granny Glasses, $65
Can be found with Skipper Skimmy Stripes #1956 and Skipper Young Ideas #1513.

White Plastic Sunglasses with Orange Stripe, $95
Can be found with Francie Clam Diggers #1258.

Red Rose Round Sunglasses, $35
Can be found with Barbie Goodies Galore #1518, Barbie Sun Set Accessories #1497, Barbie Good Sports #3351, Francie Pink Lightning #1231, Skipper Fun Runners #3372, Francie Zig Zag Zoom #3445, Francie Midi Bouquet #3446, and Francie Ready! Set! Go! #3365.

White Plastic Sunglasses with Green Stripe, $85
Can be found with Francie Gad-Abouts #1250 and Francie Clam Diggers #1258.

Blue Round Sunglasses, $25
Can be found with Barbie Goodies Galore #1518 and Barbie Sun Set Accessories #1497.

Orange Plastic Sunglasses with Green Stripe, $45
Can be found with Francie Clam Diggers #1258.

Pink Round Sunglasses, $15
Can be found with Barbie Goodies Galore #1518, Barbie Sun Set Accessories #1497, Francie Zig Zag Zoom #3445, and Francie Summer Number #3454.

Gray, Black, and Red Stripe Tie, $15
Can be found with Ken Saturday Date #786.

Burgundy Bow Tie, $15
Can be found with Ken Tuxedo #787 and Barbie Wedding Party Gift Set #1017.

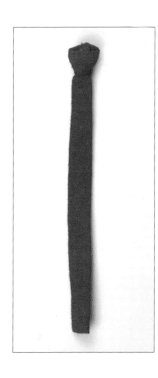

Red Tie, $15
Can be found with Ken Accessory Pak, Ken Shirt and Tie, Ken Special Date, Ken Victory Dance #1411, Ken White Is Right (pak), and Ken Seein' The Sights #1421.

Black Cotton Tie, $25
Can be found with Ken Sailor #796.

Navy Tie, $25
Can be found with Ken Army and Air Force #797 and Ken American Airlines Captain #779.

Brown Tie, $25
Can be found with Ken Army and Air Force #797 and Barbie College Student #1416.

Red Tie (shown with Ken's tie, Ricky's tie is shorter), $35
Can be found with Ricky Saturday Show #1502.

Black Ribbon Tie, $45
Can be found with Ken in Mexico #778.

Gray Silk Ascot Tie, $125
Can be found with Ken Here Comes The Groom #1426.

White Bow Tie, $95
Can be found with Ken Trousseau Set #864.

Red Bow Tie, $95
Can be found with Ken Best Man #1425.

Yellow Satin Tie, $65
Can be found with Barbie See-Worthy #1872.

Olive Tie, $85
Can be found with Ken Summer Job #1422.

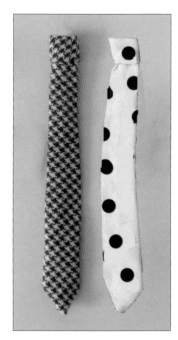

Black and White Wide Tie, $20
Black and White Polka Dot Tie $45
Can be found with Ken The VIP Scene #1473.

Orange with Yellow Dots Cotton Wide Tie, $45
Can be found with Ken Casual All Stars #1514.

Burgundy Wide Tie, $15
Can be found with Ken Cool n' Casual #3379.

Solid Fuchsia Tie, $25
Can be found with Ken Casual All Stars #1514.

Multicolor Stripe Wide Tie, $15
Can be found with Ken Casual All Stars #1514.

Multicolor Wide Tie, $15
Can be found with Ken Casual All Stars #1514 and Ken Big Business #1434.

Multicolor Silk Tie (same fabric as Barbie Outdoor Art Show), $75
Can be found with Ken Casual All Stars #1514.

Aqua Satin Tie with Necktie Ring (price includes dress), $65
Can be found with Francie Land Ho! #1220.

Yellow Cotton Wide Tie, $20
Can be found with Ken Brown On Brown #1718.

Multi Colored Tie $35
Can be found with Red, White & Wild #1589.

Yellow Tie with Black Dots, $45 (not shown)
Can be found with Red, White & Wild #1589.

White Fabric Flower Corsage, $15
Can be found with Ken Tuxedo #787.

White Flowers and Satin Bow Corsage, $25
Can be found with Barbie Finishing Touches (pak).

Metal Pilot Wings Pin, $35
Can be found with Ken Army and Air Force #797, Barbie American Airlines Stewardess #984, and Ken American Airlines Captain #779.

Metal Pan American Emblem, $75
Can be found with Barbie Pan American Airways Stewardess #1678.

Brown Muff, $15
Can be found with Barbie Winter Wow #1486.

White Plush Muff with Velvet Handle, $35 (front)
Can be found with Barbie Miss America Royal Velvet #3215 (left) and Francie Waltz in Velvet #1768 (right).

White Plush Muff with Velvet Handle, $35 (back)
Can be found with Barbie Miss America Royal Velvet #3215 (left) and Francie Waltz in Velvet #1768 (right).

White Muff, $15
Can be found with Skipper Skating Fun #1908.

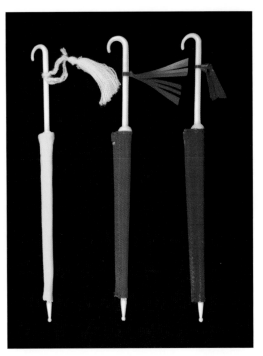

Yellow Umbrella with Tassel, $15
Can be found with Barbie Rain Coat #949, Barbie Stormy Weather #949, and Skipper Rain or Shine #1916.

Orange Umbrella with Plastic Tassel, $15
Can be found with Barbie Tour-Ins (pak) and Barbie Shoe Bag #1498.

Red Umbrella with Plastic Tassel, $15
Can be found with Barbie Fancy Trimmings (pak) and Barbie Change Abouts (pak).

Large Paper Floral Umbrella, $125
Can be found with Francie Summer Coolers #1292.

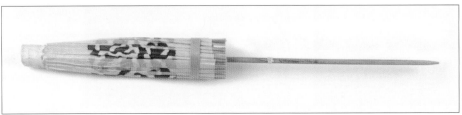

Gray Poodle, $45
Can be found with Barbie Dog n Duds #1613 and Jamie Furry Friends #1584.

White Fuzzy Cat, $275
Can be found with Barbie Kitty Capers #1062.

Pink Collar with Pink Leash, $65
Can be found with Jamie Furry Friends #1584.

White Scottie Dog, $65
Can be found with Skipper Dog Show #1929.

Red Collar with Red Leash, $25
Can be found with Skipper Dog Show #1929.

White Poodle with Blue Collar, $225
Can be found with Jamie Strollin' In Style #1247.

Beige Fuzzy Afghan Dog, $375
Can be found with Barbie Hot Togs #1063.

Brown Suede Collar with Suede Leash, $75
Can be found with Barbie Hot Togs #1063.

Aqua Collar with Gold Chain Leash, $95
Can be found with Barbie Poodle Doodles #1061.

Black Poodle, $375
Can be found with Barbie Poodle Doodles #1061.

Red Velvet Dog Coat, $15
Can be found with Barbie Dog n Duds #1613.

Plaid Dog Coat, $15
Can be found with Barbie Dog n Duds #1613.

Pink Dog Tutu, $15
Can be found with Barbie Dog n Duds #1613.

White Shaggy Dog, $65
Can be found with Tutti Me & My Dog #3554.

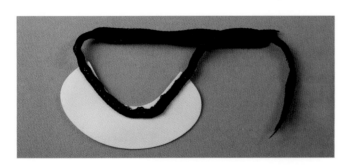

White Collar with Black Tie, $15
Can be found with Barbie Dog n Duds #1613.

Masquerade Hat, $20
Can be found with Barbie Dog n Duds #1613.

Ear Muffs, $15
Can be found with Barbie Dog n Duds #1613.

Dog Food in Yellow Bowl, $45
Can be found with Jamie Furry Friends #1584.

Dog Food in White Bowl, $20
Can be found with Barbie Dog n Duds #1613.

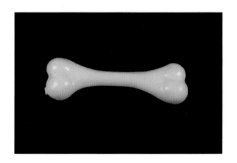

Dog Bone, $20
Can be found with Barbie Dog n Duds #1613 and Jamie Furry Friends #1584.

Red Collar with Chain Leash, $20
Can be found with Barbie Dog n Duds #1613.

Dog Food Box, $25
Can be found with Barbie Dog n Duds #1613, Jamie Furry Friends #1584, and Skipper Dog Show #1929.

Red Collar with Red Leash, $15
Can be found with Barbie Dog n Duds #1613.

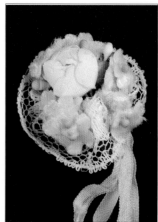

Large Floral Bouquet with Pink and White Flowers, $20
Can be found with Barbie Wedding Day Set #972.

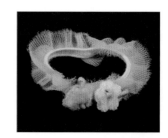

Light Blue Garter, $15
Can be found with Barbie Wedding Day Set #972, Barbie Brides Dream #947, Barbie Wedding Party Gift Set #1017, Barbie Here Comes The Bride #1665, and Barbie Beautiful Bride #1698.

Floral Bouquet with Pink and White Flowers, $20
Can be found with Barbie Brides Dream #947 and Barbie Wedding Party Gift Set #1017.

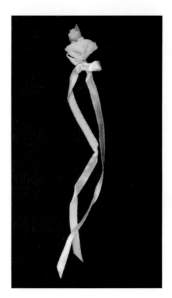

Floral Bouquet with White, Yellow, and Pink Flowers, $15
Can be found with Barbie Orange Blossom #987, Skipper Flower Girl #1904, and Barbie Wedding Party Gift Set #1017.

White Floral Bouquet with Dotted Sheer Wrap, $65
Can be found with Barbie Wedding Wonder #1849.

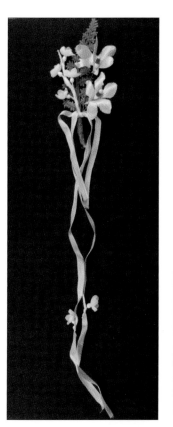

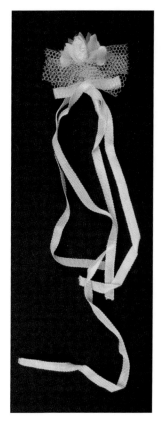

White Floral Bouquet with Pearl Centers, $65
Can be found with Barbie Beautiful Bride #1698.

Pink Flowers with White Lace and Green Trim, $25
Can be found with Barbie Winter Wedding #1880.

Tall Floral Bouquet with Plastic Fern, $145
Can be found with Barbie Here Comes The Bride #1665.

Pink Flowers with Green Trim, $25
Can be found with Barbie Winter Wedding #1880.

Pink Pom Floral Bouquet, $35
Can be found with Barbie Sweetheart Satin #3361.

Pink Flowers with White Tulle, $25
Can be found with Barbie Winter Wedding #1880.

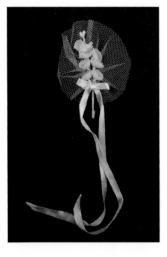

White Floral Bouquet with Green Tulle, $45
Can be found with Barbie Bridal Brocade #3417.

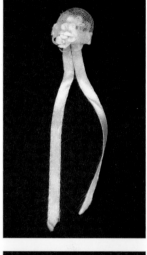

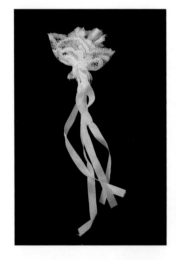
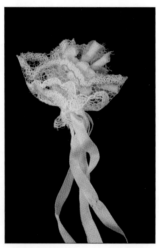

Floral Bouquet of Lilies with Green Trimmed Lace, $45
Can be found with Francie Dreamy Wedding #1217.

White Floral Bouquet with Green Tulle, $45
Can be found with Francie Victorian Wedding #1233.

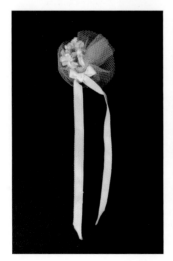
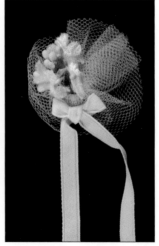

White Floral Bouquet with Green Plastic Trim, $35
Can be found with Francie Wedding Whirl #1244.

Red Roses with Ferns Bouquet, $175
Can be found with Barbie Campus Sweetheart #1616.

Tulip Bouquet, $25
Can be found with Ken In Holland #777.

White Daisy Flowers with Pink Ribbon, $25
Can be found with Barbie In Switzerland #822.

Floral Basket with Yellow Handle, $45 (Note: Tutti Basket sometimes found with less flowers.)
Can be found with Francie Bridal Beauty #3288 and Tutti Flower Girl #3615.

Single Flower with Ribbon Bouquet, $15
Can be found with Barbie Satin n' Shine #3493.

Pink Basket Filled with Flowers, $65
Can be found with Skipper Junior Bridesmaid #1934.

Bouquet of Red Satin Roses with Miss America Streamer, $65
Can be found with Majestic Blue #3216.

OPEN TOE SHOES

*T*his was the first style of shoes for Barbie doll and her friends. During the first year of production this shoe was made with a hole to accommodate Barbie dolls' stands and the corresponding holes in her feet. These shoes are found with Barbie doll outfits that are tagged ™; later the tags were marked with ®.

Within a pair only one shoe is marked "Japan" on the bottom.

 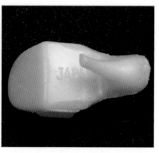

Red Open Toe Shoes, $10
Can be found with Barbie Red Flare #939, Barbie Red Silk Sheath (pak), Barbie Red Gathered Skirt (pak), Shoe Pak, Shoe Wardrobe (pak), Color Coordinates (pak), Barbie In Mexico #0820, Barbie's Hostess Set #1034, Barbie Sew-Free Fashion-Fun From Nine To Five #1703, Barbie Junior Prom #1614, Barbie Campus Sweetheart, Barbie Lunch Date (pak), Barbie Shoe Wardrobe #1833, Barbie Benefit Performance #1667, Fancy Trimmings (pak), and Barbie Original Red Swimsuit Outfit #850.

White Open Toe Shoes, $10
Can be found with Barbie Cotton Casual #912, Barbie Barbie-Q #962, Barbie Suburban Shopper #969, Barbie Wedding Day Set #972, Barbie Sheath Sensation #986, Barbie Orange Blossom #987, Barbie Registered Nurse #991, Barbie Doll Accessories #923, Barbie Garden Party #931, Barbie White Silk Sheath (pak), Barbie Fashion Queen Original Outfit, Midge Original Pink & Red Swimsuit Outfit, Midge Original Light Blue & Blue Swimsuit Outfit, Midge Original Yellow & Orange Swimsuit Outfit, Barbie Orange Blossom #987, Barbie Brides Dream #947, Barbie Busy Morning #956, Shoe Pak, Barbie Going To The Ball (pak), Barbie Costume Completers (pak), Barbie Campus Belle (pak), Barbie Crisp n' Cool #1604, Barbie Garden Tea Party #1606, Barbie White Magic #1607, Barbie In Switzerland #822, Barbie Sew-Free Fashion-Fun Sightseeing, Barbie Sew-Free Fashion-Fun Stardust #1722, Barbie Shoe Wardrobe #1833, and Barbie Flats n' Heels (pak).

Deep Blue Open Toe Shoes, $65
Can be found with Barbie Gay Parisienne #964.

Navy Open Toe Shoes, $35
Can be found with Barbie Commuter Set #916, Barbie Busy Gal #981, and Barbie Lamé Sheath (pak).

Brown Open Toe Shoes, $25
Can be found with Barbie Golden Girl #911, Barbie Peachy Fleecy Coat #915, Barbie Evening Splendour #961, Barbie Sorority Meeting #937, Barbie Golden Elegance #992, Barbie Shoe Pak, Barbie Sew-Free Fashion-Fun Day In Town #1712, Barbie Saturday Matinee #1615, and Barbie Shoe Wardrobe #1833.

Clear Open Toe Shoe with Gold Glitter, $65
Can be found with Barbie Enchanted Evening #983, Barbie Party Date #958, Barbie Sew-Free Fashion-Fun Golden Ball #1724, Barbie Shoe Wardrobe #1833, Barbie Golden Glory #1645, Barbie Pink Formal #1681, and Barbie Glimmer Glamour #1547.

Green Open Toe Shoe with Pearl, $35
Can be found with Senior Prom #951.

Black Open Toe Shoes, $10
Can be found with Barbie Apple Print Sheath #917, Barbie Cruise Stripes #918, Barbie Roman Holiday #968, Barbie Easter Parade #971, Barbie Sweater Girl #976, Barbie Silken Flame #977, Barbie Let's Dance #978, Barbie Friday Night Date #979, Barbie Solo In The Spotlight #982, Barbie American Airlines Stewardess #984, Barbie Doll Accessories #923, Barbie After Five #934, Barbie Black Silk Sheath (pak), Barbie Black Gathered Skirt (pak), Barbie Black & White Gathered Skirt (pak), Barbie Career Girl #954, Barbie Swingin' Easy #955, Barbie Black Magic #1609, Barbie Sew-Free Fashion-Fun Debutante Party #1711, Barbie Sew-Free Fashion-Fun Day n' Night #1723, and Barbie Shoe Wardrobe #1833.

Green Open Toe Shoes, $15
Can be found with Barbie Green Silk Sheath (pak), Barbie Theatre Date #959, Barbie Knit Accessories Hat & Purse (pak), Barbie Shoe Pak, Barbie Theatre Date (no hat) #1612, Barbie Shoe Wardrobe #1833, and Barbie Flats n' Heels (pak).

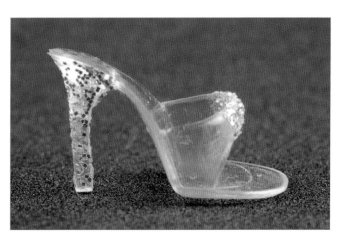

Clear Open Toe with Silver Glitter, $65
Can be found with Barbie White Satin Slacks (pak), White Satin Wrap Skirt (pak), Black Satin Wrap Skirt (pak), Barbie Black Satin Slacks (pak), Shoe Pak, Barbie Cinderella #872, Barbie Sew-Free Fashion-Fun Moonlight n' Roses #1721, Barbie Invitation To Tea #1632, Barbie Debutante Ball #1666, and Francie The Silver Cage #1208.

Light Pink Open Toe Shoes, $15
Can be found with Barbie Plantation Belle #966, Barbie Doll Accessories #923, Barbie Pink Gathered Skirt (pak), Barbie Sophisticated Lady #993, Barbie Knitting Pretty Pink #957, Barbie Magnificence #1646, Barbie Shoe Wardrobe #1833, Barbie Pink Moonbeams #1694, Barbie Lovely n' Lavender #3358, and Barbie Sparkling Pink Gift Set.

Light Pink with Glitter Open Toe Shoes, $45
Can be found with Barbie Rose Satin Slacks (pak), Barbie Pink with Glitter Satin Slacks (pak), and Barbie Shoe Pak.

Blue Open Toe Shoes, $10
Can be found with Barbie Color Coordinates (pak).

Hot Pink Open Toe Shoes, $15
Can be found with Barbie Fraternity Dance #1638, Barbie Pink Sparkle #1440, Barbie Flats n' Heels (pak), Barbie Underliners #1821, Barbie Jump Into Lace #1823, and Barbie Shoe Bag #1498.

Aqua Open Toe Shoes, $15
Can be found with Barbie Turquoise Silk Sheath (pak), Shoe Pak, Barbie Flats n' Heels (pak), Barbie Firelights #1481, and Barbie American Girl Original Outfit #1070.

Rose Pink with Glitter Open Toe Shoes, $65
Can be found with Barbie Satin n' Rose #1611.

Yellow Open Toe Shoes, $15
Can be found with Barbie Light Yellow Silk Sheath (pak), Color Coordinates (pak), Color Magic Mixer Set, Barbie Night Clouds #1841, and Barbie Leisure Leopard #1479.

Royal Blue Open Toe Shoes, $10
Can be found with Barbie Knitting Pretty Blue #957, Barbie Knit Separates #1602, Barbie Midnight Blue #1617, Barbie Shoe Wardrobe #1833, and Barbie Nite Lightning #1591.

Mustard Yellow Open Toe Shoes, $15
Can be found with Barbie Gold Yellow Silk Sheath (pak), Shoe Pak, Barbie Golden Evening #1610, and Barbie Shoe Wardrobe #1833.

White Open Toe Shoe with White Pompon, $25
Can be found with Barbie Lovely Lingerie (pak).

Orange Open Toe Shoes, $10
Can be found with Barbie Orange Gathered Skirt (pak), Shoe Pak, Color Coordinates (pak), and Barbie Shoe Wardrobe #1833.

White Open Toe Shoe with Tangerine Pompon, $65
Can be found with Barbie Dreamland #1669.

Pink Open Toe Shoe with Blue Pompon, $65
Can be found with Barbie Slumber Party #1642 and Sleepytime Gal #1674.

Light Blue Open Toe with Pompon, $45
Can be found with Barbie Sweet Dreams #973, Barbie Sleeping Pretty #1636, and Barbie Lovely Lingerie (pak).

Rose Open Toe Shoes, $20
Can be found with Barbie Fraternity Dance #1638 and Miss Barbie Original Outfit #1060.

Clear Open Toe Shoes, $25
Can be found with Silver Sparkle #1885.

Light Pink Open Toe Shoes with Pink Pompon, $25
Can be found with Barbie Lovely Lingerie (pak) and Nighty Negligee Set #965.

Black Open Toe Shoes with Yellow Pompon, $45
Can be found with Barbie Masquerade #944.

Yellow Terry Cloth Slippers, $15
Can be found with Barbie Singin' In The Shower #988 and Barbie Bathrobe (pak).

Blue Terry Cloth Slippers, $10
Can be found with Ken Terry Togs #784 and Ken Morning Workout (pak).

Blue Terry Cloth Slippers, $25
Can be found with Ricky Lights Out #1501 (smaller than Ken's).

Coral Satin and Blue Nylon Slippers, $25
Can be found with Barbie Cloud 9 #1489.

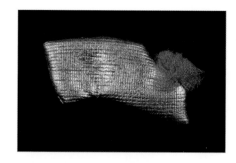

Gold Lamé Slippers with Pink Pouf, $25
Can be found with Julia Pink Fantasy #1754.

Hot Pink Felt Slipper with Light Pink Flower, $15
Can be found with Barbie Dreamy Pink #1857 and Barbie Petti-Pinks (pak).

Pink Fuzzy Slipper with Pink Bow, $15
Can be found with Barbie Lovely-Sleep Ins #1463.

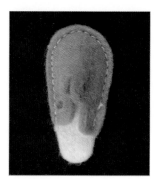

Pink Felt Slippers with White Soles, $15
Can be found with Barbie Dreamy Wrap #1476.

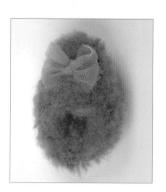

Pink Fuzzy Slipper with Hot Pink Bow, $15
Can be found with Barbie Baby Doll Pinks #3403.

White Felt Slippers with Pink Pouf, $15
Can be found with Barbie Sleepy Set #3487 and Francie Rise and Shine #1194 (sometimes found with a smaller pouf).

Yellow Felt Slippers with White Button, $45
Can be found with Francie Pretty Power #1512.

White Felt Slippers with Blue Satin and Lace, $25
Can be found with Barbie The Dream Team #3427.

White Felt Slippers with Hot Pink Pouf, $45
Can be found with Francie Snappy Snoozers #1238.

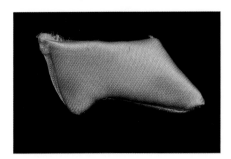

Light Blue Satin Slippers, $15
Can be found with Barbie Satin Slumber #3414.

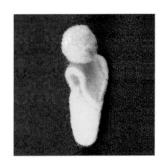

Yellow Felt Slipper with Pink Pompon, $15
Can be found with Francie Slumber Number #1271.

White Nylon Slippers Shoes with Lace Trim, $15
Can be found with Light n' Lazy #3339.

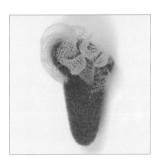

Orange Felt Slipper with Orange Poufs, $20
Can be found with Francie Snooze News #1226.

Pink Felt Bootie Slippers with Gold Bead, $15
Can be found with Barbie Sweet Dreams #3350.

Aqua Felt Bootie Slippers with Gold Bead, $25
Can be found with Francie Sleepy Time Gal #3364.

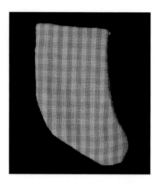

Blue and White Check Bootie Slipper, $15
Can be found with Francie Tuckered Out #1253.

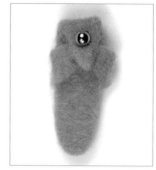

Pink Felt Slipper with Silver Bead, $35
Can be found with Francie Snooze News #3453.

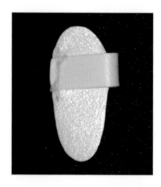

White Vinyl Slipper Scuff, $45
Can be found with Francie Little Knits #3275.

Aqua Felt Slipper with White Trim, $25
Can be found with Skipper Loungin' Lovelies #1930.

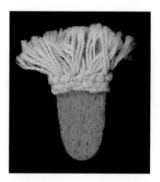

Pink Felt Slippers with Pink Fringe, $15
Can be found with Skipper Dreamtime #1909.

Hot Pink Felt Scuffs, $25
Can be found with Skipper Jamas n' Jaunties #1944.

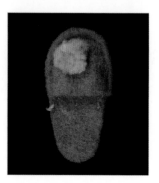

Hot Pink Felt Slippers with Pink and Blue Pouf, $25
Can be found with Skipper Baby Dolls #1957.

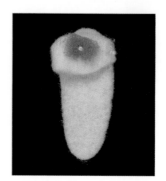

Pink Felt Slipper with Coral Pouf, $15
Can be found with Skipper Jazzy Jamys #1967.

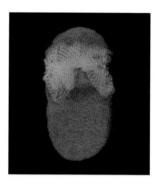

Hot Pink Slipper with Lime Green Trim, $20
Can be found with Skipper Lullaby Lime #3473.

Yellow Felt Slippers with Yellow Poufs, $25
Can be found with Skipper Nighty Nice (pak).

Yellow Fuzzy Bootie Slippers, $20
Can be found with Skipper Lemon Fluff #1749.

Brown Slippers, $15
Can be found with Ken Breakfast At 7 #1428 and Ken Sun Fun (pak).

Yellow Slippers with Sheer Yellow Bow, $45
Can be found with Skipper Dream Ins #3293 (yellow version).

Pink Scuff Slippers with Lace Trim, $20
Can be found with Tutti Night Night Sleep Tight #3553.

Hot Pink Slippers with Sheer Pink Bow, $25
Can be found with Skipper Dream Ins #3293 (pink version).

Pink Felt Scuff Slippers, $15
Can be found with Tutti Pinky P.J.'s #3616.

Yellow Felt Bootie Slippers with Gold Bead, $20
Can be found with Skipper Super Snoozers #3371.

Red Fuzzy Slippers, $35
Can be found with Ken Off To Bed #1413.

SKATES

White Ice Skates, $15
Can be found with Barbie Icebreaker #942, Barbie Skater's Waltz #1629, Barbie Skate Mates #1793, Francie Sportin' Set #1044, and Skipper Ice Skatin' #3470.

Aqua Ice Skates, $25
Can be found with Barbie Action Accents #1585.

Black Ice Skates, $15
Can be found with Ken Fun On Ice #791 and Ken Shoes For Sport (pak).

Red Roller Skates, $25
Can be found with Skipper On Wheels #1032 and Skipper Just For Fun (pak).

White Roller Skates, $15
Can be found with Barbie For Rink and Court (pak) and Barbie Goodies Galore #1518.

White Ice Skates, $15
Can be found with Skipper Skating Fun #1908 and Skipper Just For Fun (pak).

Red Ice Skates, $15
Can be found with Barbie For Rink and Court (pak) and Barbie Goodies Galore #1518.

Brown Roller Skates with White Wheels, $15
Can be found with Ken Roller Skate #1405 and Ken Shoes For Sport (pak).

Red Roller Skate with Clear Strap, $95
Can be found with Skipper Rolla Scoot #1940.

KEN & RICKY SHOES

Black Dress Shoes, $8
Can be found with Ken Saturday Date #786, Ken Tuxedo #787, Ken The Yachtsman #789, Ken Masquerade #794, Ken Sailor #796, Ken Special Date #1401, Ken American Airlines Captain #779, Ken Best Foot Forward (pak), Barbie's Wedding Party Gift Set #1017, Ken Rovin' Reporter #1417, Ken Here Comes The Groom #1426, Ken Seein' The Sights #1421, Ken Summer Job #1422, Ken A Go Go #1423, and Ken Best Man #1425.

Black and White Dress Shoes, $10
Can be found with Ken Victory Dance #1411, Ken Best Foot Forward (pak), Ken White is Right (pak), and Ken Holiday #1414.

Brown and White Dress Shoes, $10
Can be found with Ken Casuals #782, Ken Accessory Pak, and Ken Best Foot Forward (pak).

Brown Dress Shoes, $8
Can be found with Ken Sport Shorts #783, Ken Dreamboat #785, Ken Accessory Pak, Ken Army and Air Force #797, Ken Best Foot Forward (pak), Ken Hiking Holiday #1412, and Ken College Student #1416.

Light Brown Dress Shoes, $10
Can be found with Ken Best Foot Forward (pak).

Navy Dress Shoes, $20
Can be found with Ken Army and Air Force #797.

White Dress Shoes, $10
Can be found with Ken Campus Hero #770, Dr. Ken #793, Ken Drum Major #775, Ken Best Foot Forward (pak), and Ken Mountain Hike #1427.

White Tennis Shoes, $10
Can be found with Ken Time For Tennis #790, Ken Shoes For Sports (pak), Ken Going Bowling #1403, and Ken Jazz Concert #1420.

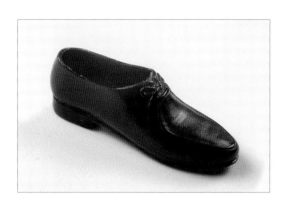

Black High Top Hiking Shoes
Can be found with Ken Boxing (pak) and Ken In Switzerland #776.

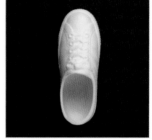

White Tennis Shoes (larger than the earlier version), $8
Can be found with Ken Denims For Fun #3376 and Ken Red, White and Wild #1829.

Black Ski Boots, $10
Can be found with Ken Hunting Shirt (pak), Ken Ski Champion #798, Ken Going Hunting #1409, and Ken Shoes For Sports (pak).

White Tennis Shoes for Ricky and Skipper, $15
Can be found with Ricky Little Leaguer #1504, Ricky Skateboard Set #1505, and Skipper Fun Runners #3372.

Black Tennis Shoes for Ricky, $15
Can be found with Ricky Saturday Show #1502, Ricky Sunday Suit #1503, and Ricky Let's Explore #1506.

Navy Ski Boots, $15
Can be found with Ken The Skiing Scene #1438.

Black Cleats, $10
Can be found with Ken Touchdown #799, Ken Play Ball #792, and Ken Shoes For Sports (pak).

Black Cowboy Boots, $15
Can be found with Ken In Mexico #778.

Brown Cowboy Boots, $15
Can be found with Ken Rally Gear #1429, Ken Shoe Ins (pak), Ken Way Out West #1720, Ken Beach Beat #3384, and Ken Western Winner #3378.

Brown Loafer Shoes, $10
Can be found with Ken Play It Cool #1433, Ken Bold Gold #1436, Ken Casual All Stars #1514, Ken The Suede Scene #1439, Ken Shoe Ins (pak), Ken Casual Cords v#1717, and Ken Brown On Brown #1718.

Navy Loafer Shoes, $45
Can be found with Ken Red, White and Wild #1589.

Blue Sandals, $10
Can be found with Allan Original Outfit #1000.

Orange Sandals, $25
Can be found with Ken In Hawaii #1404.

Red Sandals for Ricky, $10
Can be found with Ricky Original Outfit.

Red Sandals, $8
Can be found with Ken Original Outfit and Ken T.V.'s Good Tonight #1419.

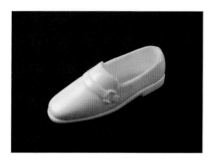

White Loafer Shoes, $15
Can be found with Ken Fabulous Formal Gift Set #1595, Ken Town Turtle #1430, Ken Guruvy Formal #1431, Ken The Sea Scene #1449, and Ken Shoe Ins (pak).

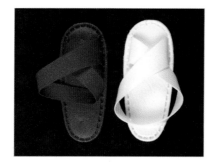

Burgundy Sandals, $15
Can be found with Ken Mod Madras #1828.

White Sandals, $15
Can be found with Ken The Casual Scene #1472, Ken Shoe Ins (pak), Ken Wide Awake Stripes #3377, and Ken Beach Beat #3384.

Black Loafer Shoes, $15
Can be found with Big Business #1434, The V.I.P. Scene #1473, Ken The Night Scene #1496, Ken Shoe Ins (pak), Ken Midnight Blue #1719, Ken Beach Beat #3384, and Ken Cool n' Casual #3379.

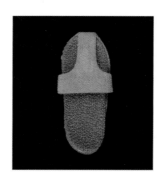

Tan Suede Sandals, $95
Can be found with Ken Surf's Up #1248.

Red Closed Toe Shoes, $15
Can be found with Barbie Student Teacher #1622, Barbie Aboard Ship #1631, Barbie Matinee Fashion #1640, Barbie Red Delight (pak), Barbie Match Mates (pak), Barbie Music Center Matinee #1663, Barbie Shimmering Magic #1664, Barbie Travel Togethers #1688, Barbie Studio Tour #1690, Barbie Fashion Shiner #1691, Barbie Flats n' Heels (pak), Barbie Evening Enchantment #1695, Barbie Floating Gardens #1696, Barbie Best Bow (pak), Barbie Fancy Trimmings (pak), Barbie Glo-Go #1865, and Barbie Shoe Bag #1498.

Red Closed Toe Spike Shoes, $65
Can be found with Barbie Student Teacher #1622, Barbie Aboard Ship #1631, Barbie Matinee Fashion #1640, Barbie Red Delight (pak), Barbie Music Center Matinee #1663, and Barbie Shimmering Magic #1664.

Clear Closed Toe Spike Shoes (pair), $175
Can be found with Ken The Prince #772.

Clear Closed Toe Shoes (pair), $75
Can be found with Ken The Prince #772.

Orange Closed Toe Shoes, $15
Can be found with Barbie Brunch Time #1628, Barbie Match Mates (pak), Barbie Flats n' Heels (pak), Barbie Tropicana #1460, Barbie Bouncy Flouncy #1805, Barbie Disco Dater #1807, Barbie Goldswinger #1494, and Barbie Shoe Bag #1498.

Light Pink Closed Toe Shoes, $25
Can be found with Barbie Flats n' Heels (pak) and Barbie Fashion Luncheon #1656.

Bone Closed Toe Shoes, $15
Can be found with Barbie On The Avenue #1644, Barbie Flats n' Heels (pak), Barbie London Tour #1661, and Barbie Sunday Visit #1675.

Translucent Orange Closed Toes Shoes, $20
Can be found with Barbie Brunch Time #1628, Barbie Match Mates (pak), Barbie Flats n' Heels (pak), Barbie Tropicana #1460, Barbie Bouncy Flouncy #1805, Barbie Disco Dater #1807, Barbie Goldswinger #1494, and Barbie Shoe Bag #1498.

Rose Pink Closed Toe Shoes, $35
Can be found with Barbie Disc Date #1633, Barbie Garden Wedding #1658, and Barbie Red Fantastic #1817.

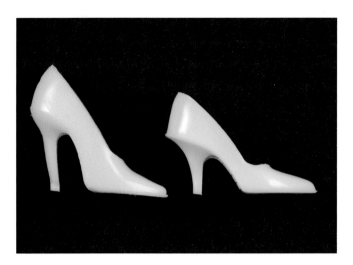

White Closed Toe Spike Shoes, $45
Can be found with Barbie Dancing Doll #1626, Barbie Country Club Dance #1627, and Barbie Holiday Dance #1639.

White Closed Toe Shoes, $15
Can be found with Barbie Dancing Doll #1626, Barbie Country Dance #1627, Barbie Holiday Dance #1639, Barbie Match Mates (pak), Barbie International Fair #1653, Barbie Here Comes The Bride #1665, Barbie Intrigue #1470, Barbie Formal Occasion #1697, Barbie Beautiful Bride #1698, Barbie Skirt Styles (pak), Barbie Wedding Wonder #1849, Barbie Midi-Marvelous #1870, Barbie Winter Wedding #1880, and Barbie Terrific Twosome (pak).

Brown Closed Toe Shoes, $75
Can be found with Barbie Gold n' Glamour #1647.

Hot Pink Closed Toe Shoes, $15
Can be found with Barbie Sunflower #1683, Barbie Print Aplenty #1686, Barbie Red Fantastic #1817, Barbie Dinner Dazzle #1551, Barbie Silver n' Satin #1552, Barbie Swirly Cue #1822, Barbie Dancing Stripes #1843, Barbie Extravaganza #1844, Barbie Scene Stealers #1845, Barbie Team-ups #1855, Extra-Casuals (pak), Barbie Happy Go Pink #1868, Barbie Romantic Ruffles #1871, Barbie Fab City #1874, and Barbie Shoe Bag #1498.

Brown Closed Toe Spike Shoes, $145
Can be found with Barbie Gold n' Glamour #1647.

Navy Blue Closed Toe Shoes, $95
Can be found with Barbie Patio Party #1692.

Royal Blue Closed Toe Shoes, $15
Can be found with Barbie Barbie Match Mates (pak), Patio Party #1692, Barbie Fancy Trimmings (pak), Barbie Stacey Nite Lightning #1591, and Barbie Shoe Bag #1498.

Blue Closed Toe Shoes, $25
Can be found with Barbie Twinkle Togs #1854, Change Abouts (pak), and Barbie Shoe Bag #1498.

Green Closed Toe Spike Shoes, $145
Can be found with Barbie Junior Designer #1620 and Barbie Modern Art #1625.

Olive Green Closed Toe Shoes, $175
Can be found with Barbie Poodle Parade #1643.

Green Closed Toe Shoes, $25
Can be found with Barbie Junior Designer #1620, Barbie Modern Art #1625, Barbie Poodle Parade #1643, and Barbie Dressed-up! (pak).

Coral Pink Closed Toe Shoes, $25
Can be found with Barbie Red Fantastic #1817.

Deep Blue Closed Toe Shoes, $65
Can be found with Barbie Beautiful Blues #3303.

Black Closed Toe Shoes, $15
Can be found with Barbie Flats n' Heels (pak), Barbie Pretty As A Picture #1652, Barbie Pan American Airways Stewardess #1678, Barbie Pretty Power #1868, Barbie Midi-Magic #1869, and Barbie Shoe Bag #1498.

Olive Green Closed Toe Spike Shoes, $95
Can be found with Barbie Poodle Parade #1643.

Light Blue Closed Toe Spike Shoes, $125
Can be found with Barbie Learns To Cook #1635 and Barbie Reception Line #1654.

Light Blue Closed Toe Shoes, $15
Can be found with Barbie Learns To Cook #1635, Barbie Reception Line #1654, and Barbie Knit Hit #1804.

Aqua Closed Toe Spike Shoes, $65
Can be found with Barbie Fashion Editor #1635.

Aqua Closed Toe Shoes, $15
Can be found with Barbie Fashion Editor #1635, Barbie Flats n' Heels (pak), Barbie Club Meeting #1672, Barbie Let's Have A Ball #1879, and Barbie Shoe Bag #1498.

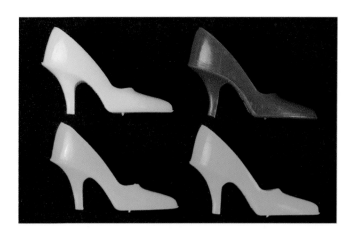

Yellow Closed Toe Shoes, $175
Can be found with Barbie Shoe Bag #1498.

Grape Closed Toe Shoes, $150
Can be found with Barbie Shoe Bag #1498.

Lime Green Closed Toe Shoes (aka Acid Green), $225
Can be found with Barbie Shoe Bag #1498.

Apple Green Closed Toe Shoes, $175
Can be found with Barbie Shoe Bag #1498.

WEDGE SHOES

White Cork Wedge Shoes, $15
Can be found with Barbie Resort Set #963 and Barbie Winter Holiday #975.

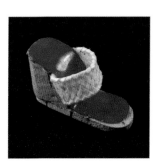

Woven Strap and Red Insole Wedge Shoes, $35
Can be found with Barbie Picnic Set #967.

Gold Cork Wedge Shoes, $25
Can be found with Barbie Mood For Music #940, Barbie Helena Swimsuit (pak), and Barbie Dinner At Eight #946.

Blue and Brown Wedge Shoes, $25
Can be found with Barbie Blue Knit Slacks (pak), Barbie Shoe Pak (pak), and Barbie Shoe Wardrobe #1833.

Red and Brown Wedge Shoes, $25
Can be found with Barbie Stripe Knit Slacks (pak).

Blue with Blue Wedge Shoes, $15
Can be found with Barbie In Blooms #3424.

Orange Wedge Shoes with Ankle Ties, $45
Can be found with Barbie Peasant Pleasant #3482.

Red Cork Wedge Shoes, $35
Can be found with Barbie Open Road #985.

Yellow Gold and Tan Wedge Shoes, $15
Can be found with Barbie Yellow Gold Knit Slacks (pak) and Barbie Flat's n' Heels #1837.

Courtesy of Marl & B

Gold and Brown Wedge Shoes, $15
Can be found Barbie Flat's n' Heels #183, and (pak) Barbie Shoe Wardrobe #1833, Barbie In The Swim (pak)

PILGRIM SHOES

Hot Pink Pilgrim Shoes, $8
Can be found with Barbie Silver 'n Satin #1552, Barbie Little Bow-Pink #1483, Barbie Pink Premiere #1596, Barbie Pink Fantasy #1754, Barbie Make Mine Midi #1861, Barbie Movie Groovy #1866, Barbie Happy Go Pink #1868, Barbie Romantic Ruffles #1871, Barbie Fab City #1874, Barbie Flats 'n Heels (pak), Barbie Special Sparkle #1468, Barbie Glamour Group #1510, Barbie Goodies Galore #1518, Barbie Ruffles 'n Swirls (Pink Version) #1783, Barbie The Lace Caper #1791, Barbie Sharp Shift (pak), Cool Casuals (pak), Barbie Foot Lights (pak), Barbie Glowin Out #3404, Barbie Evening In #3406, Barbie Fun Flakes #3412, Barbie Walking Pretty (pak), and Barbie Flying Colors #3492.

Navy Blue Pilgrim Shoes, $8
Can be found with Barbie Now Knit #1452 and Barbie Soft n' Snug (pak).

Royal Blue Pilgrim Shoes, $8
Can be found with Barbie Now Knit #1452 and Barbie Soft n' Snug (pak).

Purple Pilgrim Shoes, $8
Can be found with Barbie Silver Blues #3357 and Barbie Fancy That Purple #3362.

Blue Pilgrim Shoes, $8
Can be found with Dreamy Blues #1456, Gypsy Spirit #1458, Blue Royalty #1469, Goodies Galore #1518, Fashion Accents #1521, Ruffles n' Swirls (blue version) #1783, Rainbow Wraps #1798, Cool Casuals (pak), Foot Lights (pak), Strollin' In Style #1247, Majestic Blue #3216, Glowin' Gold #3354, and Shoe Scene #3382.

Fuchsia Pilgrim Shoes, $8
Can be found with Barbie Soft n' Snug (pak) and Barbie Picture Me Pretty #3355.

Aqua Pilgrim Shoes, $8
Can be found with Julia Simply Wow #1594, Julia Brrr-Furrr (blue version) #1752, Barbie Let's Have A Ball #1879, Barbie Flats n' Heels (pak), Barbie Mood Matchers #1792, and Barbie Sharp Shift (pak).

Orange Pilgrim Shoes, $10
Can be found with Barbie Fun Shine #3480, Barbie Tangerine Scene #1451, Barbie Goodies Galore #1518, and Barbie Walking Pretty (pak).

Black Pilgrim Shoes, $8
Can be found with Barbie Pretty Power #1863, Barbie Midi-Magic #1869, Barbie Goodies Galore #1518, Barbie Walking Pretty (pak), Barbie Pants-Perfect Purple #3359, Barbie Pleasantly Peasanty #3360, Barbie Shoe Scene #3382, and Barbie Long n' Fringy #3341.

Yellow Pilgrim Shoes, $8
Can be found with Barbie Hurray For Leather #1477, Barbie Leisure Leopard #1479, Barbie Important In-Vestment #1482, Barbie Yellow Mellow #1484, Barbie Shirt Dressy #1487, Barbie Silver Polish #1492, Barbie Fabulous Formal #1595, Julia Candlelight Capers #1753, Barbie Loop Scoop #1453, Barbie Great Coat #1459, Barbie Rare Pair #1462, Barbie Lemon Kick #1465, Barbie Goodies Galore #1518, Barbie Check The Suit #1794, Barbie Fur Sighted #1796, Barbie Sharp Shift (pak), Barbie Foot Lights (pak), Barbie Midi Mood #3407, Barbie Walking Pretty (pak), and Barbie Shoe Scene (pak).

Lime Green Pilgrim Shoes, $8
Can be found with Barbie Velvet Venture #1488, Barbie Flower Wower #1453, Barbie City Sparkler #1457, Barbie Goodies Galore #1518, Barbie All About Plaid #3433, Barbie Sharp Shift (pak), Barbie Walking Pretty (pak), and Barbie Foot Lights (pak).

Green Pilgrim Shoes, $8
Can be found with Barbie Important In-Vestment (green version) #1482, Barbie Cool Casuals (pak), Barbie Two Way Tiger #3402, and Barbie Walking Pretty (pak).

White Pilgrim Shoes, $8
Can be found with Barbie Midi-Marvelous #1870, Barbie Winter Wedding #1880, Barbie Flats n' Heels (pak), Barbie Glamour Group #1510, Barbie Fashion Bouquet #1511, Barbie Goodies Galore #1518, Barbie Fashion Accents #1521, Barbie Sharp Shift (pak), Barbie Foot Lights (pak), Barbie Walking Pretty (pak), Barbie White n' With It #3352, Barbie Sweetheart Satin #3361, Barbie Shoe Scene #3382, Barbie Purple Pleasers #3483, Barbie Satin n' Shine #3493, and Julia Nurse Original Outfit #1127.

Rose Pilgrim Shoes, $8
Can be found with Barbie Sharp Shift (pak) and Barbie Royal Velvet #3215.

Red Pilgrim Shoes, $8
Can be found with Barbie Shift Into Knit #1478, Barbie Mad About Plaid Gift Set #1587, Julia Brrr-Furrr (red version) #1752, Barbie Goodies Galore #1518, Barbie Sharp Shift (pak), Barbie Soft n' Snug (pak), Barbie Walking Pretty (pak), Barbie All American Girl #3337, Barbie Madras Mad #3585, and Julia Leather Weather #1751.

Pink Pilgrim Shoes, $65
Can be found with Straight Leg Truly Scrumptious original outfit and Talking Truly Scrumptious original outfit.

T-STRAP SHOES

Clear T-Strap Shoes, $75
Can be found with Barbie Silver Sparkle #1885 (Salute To Silver Fan Club Package version can be found with Clear Open Toe Shoes).

Black T-Strap Shoes, $45
Can be found with Barbie Hair Happenin's Original Outfit #1174.

Lime Green, Green, Yellow, White, Aqua, Royal Blue, Purple, Rose, Orange, and Hot Pink

Yellow T-Strap Shoes, $15
Can be found with Barbie Loop Scoop #1454, Barbie Great Coat #1459, Barbie Lemon Kick #1465, Barbie Goodies Galore #1518, Barbie Check The Suit #1794, and Barbie Midi Mood #3407.

Green T-Strap Shoes, $15
Can be found with Barbie Flower Wower #1453, Barbie Fashion Bouquet #1511, Barbie Goodies Galore #1518, and Barbie Two-Way Tiger #3402.

Lime Green T-Strap Shoes, $15
Can be found with Barbie City Sparkler #1457 and Barbie All About Plaid #3433.

White T-Strap Shoes, $15
Can be found with Barbie Glamour Group #1510, Barbie Goodies Galore #1518, Barbie Bridal Brocade #3417, and Barbie Sweetheart Satin #3361.

Royal Blue T-Strap Shoes, $15
Can be found with Barbie Now Knit #1452, Barbie Goodies Galore #1518, and Barbie Dreamy Blues #1456.

Orange T-Strap Shoes, $15
Can be found with Barbie Goodies Galore #1518.

Aqua T-Strap Shoes, $15
Can be found with Barbie Mood Matchers #1792 and Barbie Silver Serenade #3419.

Rose T-Strap Shoes, $20
Can be found with Barbie Goodies Galore #1518, Barbie Victorian Velvet #3431 (rose version), and Barbie Dancing Lights #3437.

Blue T-Strap Shoes, $15
Can be found with Barbie Gypsy Spirit #1458, Barbie Blue Royalty #1469, Barbie Goodies Galore #1518, Barbie Ruffles n' Swirls #1783, and Barbie Rainbow Wraps #1798.

Purple T-Strap Shoes, $15
Can be found with Barbie Peasant Dressy #3438, Barbie Victorian Velvet #3431, Barbie Silver Blues #3357, and Barbie Fancy That Purple #3362.

Hot Pink T-Strap Shoes, $15
Can be found with Barbie Gypsy Spirit #1458, Barbie Special Sparkle #1468, Barbie Glamour Group #1510, Barbie Goodies Galore #1518, Barbie Ruffles n' Swirls #1783, Barbie The Lace Caper #1791, Barbie Glowin' Out #3404, Barbie Evening In #3406, Barbie Fun Flakes #3412, Barbie Victorian Velvet #3431, and Barbie Dancing Lights #3437.

SOFT POINTED HEEL SHOES

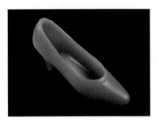

Royal Blue Pointed Heel Shoes, $75
Can be found with Barbie Travel In Style #1544.

Hot Pink Pointed Heel Shoes, $15
Can be found with Francie Sun Spots #1277, Francie Tweed-Somes #1286, Francie The Silver Cage #1208, and Francie The Combo #1215.

Yellow pointed Heel Shoes, $20
Can be found with Francie Fresh As A Daisy #1254, Francie Clam Diggers #1258, Francie In-Print #1288, Francie, Pleat Neat Pak, Francie Foot Notes Pak, and Francie Vested Interest #1224.

Light Blue Pointed Heel Shoes, $15
Can be found with Francie First Formal #1260 and Francie Miss Teenage Beauty #1284.

Aqua Pointed Heel Shoes, $15
Can be found with Francie It's A Date #1251.

Blue Pointed Heel Shoes, $15
Can be found with Francie Style Setters #1268.

Red Pointed Heel Shoes, $15
Can be found with Francie Concert In The Park #1256, Francie Check-Mates #1259, Francie Hi-Teen #1272, and Francie Side-Kick #1272 .

White Pointed Heel Shoes, $15
Can be found with Francie Iced Blue #1274, Francie Cool White #1280, Francie Sweet n' Swingin' #1283, Francie Note The Coat #1289, Francie Check This! #1291, and Francie Dreamy Wedding #1217.

Pink Pointed Heel Shoes, $15
Can be found with Francie Dance Party #1257, Francie Shoppin' Spree #1261, Francie Go Granny Go #1267, Francie Summer Frost #1276, Francie Sweet n' Swingin' #1283, Francie Partners In Print #1293, Francie Prom Pinks #1295, and Casey Goes Casual #3304.

Red Flat Shoes, $25
Can be found with Barbie Knit Hit #1621 and Barbie Perfectly Plaid #1193.

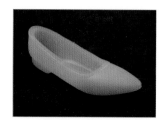

Light Pink Flat Shoes, $25
Can be found with Barbie Vacation Time #1623.

Aqua Flat Shoes, $45
Can be found with Barbie Photo Fashion #1648, Barbie Sporting Casuals #1641.

Pink Flat Shoes, $25
Can be found with Barbie Color Magic Fashion Fun #4041, Color Magic Mix n' Matchers #1779, and Barbie Flats n' Heels (pak).

Yellow Flat Shoes, $25
Can be found with Barbie Tropicana #1687, Barbie Pajama Pow! #1806, Barbie Pedal Pushers (pak), Barbie Country Caper #1862, and Francie Clam Diggers #1258.

Orange Flat Shoes, $25
Can be found with Barbie Tangerine Scene #1451.

Hot Pink Flat Shoes, $45
Can be found with Barbie Bermuda Holiday #1810, Barbie Weekenders #1815, Barbie Velvet-Teens #1818, and Barbie In Blooms #3424.

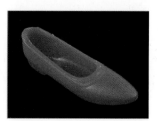

Green Flat Shoes, $20
Can be found with Francie Gad-Abouts #1250.

Blue Flat Shoes, $45
Can be found with Barbie Turtle n' Tights #3426.

POINTED HEELS CUT OUT SHOES

Red Pointed Heels with Cut Out Shoes, $15
Can be found with Francie Check-Mates #1259, Francie Hi-Teen #1272, Francie Side Kick #1273, and Francie Foot Notes (pak)

Orange Pointed Heels with Cut Out Shoes, $20
Can be found with Francie Wild n' Wooly #1218, Twiggy Twigster #1727, Francie Foot Notes (pak), and Francie Gold Rush #1222.

White Pointed Heels with Cut Out Shoes, $15
Can be found with Francie Sweet n' Swingin' #1283, Francie Note The Coat! #1289, Francie Check This! #1291, Francie Dreamy Wedding #1217, Francie Foot Notes (pak), Francie Slightly Summery (pak), Francie Victorian Wedding #1233, and Francie Wedding Whirl #1244.

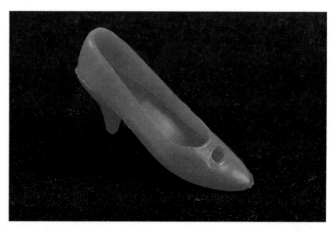

Yellow Pointed Heels with Cut Out Shoes, $20
Can be found with Barbie Extra Casuals (pak), Francie Pleat-Neat (pak), Francie In Print #1288, and Francie Vested Interest #1224.

Hot Pink Pointed Heels with Cut Out Shoes, $15
Can be found with Barbie Extra Casuals (pak), Francie Go Granny Go #1267, Francie Summer Frost #1276, Francie Sun Spots #1277, Francie Sweet n' Swingin' #1283, Francie Partners In Print #1293, Francie Prom Pinks #1295, Francie Floating-In #1207, Francie The Silver Cage #1208, Francie Foot Notes (pak), Francie Vested Interest #1224, Francie Snazz #1225, Francie Two For The Ball #1232, and Francie Altogether Elegant #1242.

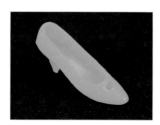

Green Pointed Heels with Cut Out Shoes, $45
Can be found with Francie Pazam! #1213.

Blue Pointed Heels with Cut Out Shoes, $65
Can be found with Francie First Formal #1260 and Francie Foot Notes (pak).

Royal Blue Bow Shoes, $15
Can be found with Barbie Mini Prints #1809, Barbie Travel In Style #1544, Barbie Stacey Nite Lightning #1591, Barbie Flats n' Heels (pak), Barbie Shoe Bag #1498, and Barbie Foot Lights (pak).

Aqua Blue Bow Shoes, $125
Can be found with Barbie The Yellow Go #1816.

White Bow Shoes, $25
Can be found with Barbie Sparkle Squares #1814 and Barbie Midi-Marvelous #1870.

Yellow Bow Shoes, $15
Can be found with Barbie Snap Dash #1824, Barbie Great Coat #1459, Barbie Rare Pair #1462, Barbie Lemon Kick #1465, and Twiggy-Do's #1725.

Hot Pink Bow Shoes, $15
Can be found with Togetherness #1842, Barbie Fancy-Dancy #1858, Barbie Little Bow-Pink #1483, Barbie Twinkle Town #1592, Barbie Make Mine Midi #1861, Barbie Movie Groovie #1866, Barbie Romantic Ruffles #1871, Barbie Flats n' Heels (pak), Barbie Bright n' Brocade #1786, Francie The Combo #1215, and Francie The Lace-Pace #1216.

Orange Bow Shoes, $25
Can be found with Barbie All That Jazz #1848, Barbie Flats n' Heels (pak), Barbie Fun Shine #3480, and Francie Mini-Chex #1209.

Red Bow Shoes, $15
Can be found with Barbie Shift Into Knit #1478 and Barbie Foot Lights (pak).

Black Bow Shoes, $15
Can be found with Barbie Pretty Power #1863, Barbie Midi-Magic #1869, and Barbie Pants-Perfect Purple #3359.

Light Blue Bow Shoes, $15
Can be found with Barbie Flats n' Heels (pak) and Barbie Foot Lights (pak).

Lime Green Bow Shoes, $15
Can be found with Barbie Tour-Ins (pak), Merry Go Rounders #1230, and Francie Tenterrific #1211.

Kelly Green Bow Shoe, $20
Can be found with Barbie Fashion Bouquet #1511.

Yellow Flat Buckle Shoes, $20
Can be found with Francie Swingin' Separates #1042, Francie Hip Knits #1265, and Francie Somethin' Else! #1219.

Royal Blue Buckle Shoes, $20
Can be found with Francie Leather Limelight #1269, Francie Bells #1275, Francie The Bridge Bit #1279, Francie Denims On! #1290, Twiggy Gear #1728, and Francie Striped Types #1243.

Hot Pink Buckle Shoes, $20
Can be found with Francie Quick Shift #1266, Francie Go Granny Go #1267, Francie Partners In Print #1293, Francie Go Gold #1294, Casey Goes Casual #3304, Francie Sissy Suits #1228, Francie Sugar Sheers #1229, Francie Pink Lightning #1231, Francie Satin Happenin' #1237, Francie Altogether Elegant #1242, and Francie Sunny Slacks #1761.

Translucent Aqua Buckle Shoes, $45
Can be found with Francie Land Ho! #1220 and Francie Bloom Zoom #1239.

Translucent Pink Buckle Shoes, $15
Can be found with Francie Quick Shift #1266, Francie Go Granny Go #1267, Francie Partners In Print #1293, Francie Go Gold #1294, Casey Goes Casual #3304, Francie Sissy Suits #1228, Francie Sugar Sheers #1229, Francie Pink Lightning #1231, Francie Satin Happenin' #1237, Francie Altogether Elegant #1242, and Francie Sunny Slacks #1761.

Orange Buckle Shoes, $35
Can be found with Francie Orange Zip #1548.

White Buckle Shoes, $145
Can be found with No Bangs Francie Original Outfit

Black Flat Buckle Shoes, $20
Can be found with Francie Fur Out #1262, Francie Border-Line #1287, and Francie Foot Notes (pak).

Light Blue Buckle Shoes, $25
Can be found with Francie Foot Notes (pak) and Francie The Yellow Bit #1223.

Aqua Buckle Shoes, $25
Can be found with Francie Leather Limelight #1269.

Red Buckle Shoes, $20
Can be found with Barbie Shape Ups #1782.

SOFT BUCKLE FLAT WITH GOLD BUCKLE

Yellow Flat Buckle Shoes with Gold Buckle, $125
Can be found with Francie Hip Knits #1265.

SOFT BUCKLE FLAT WITH SILVER BUCKLE

Black Flat Buckle Shoes with Silver Buckle, $125
Can be found with Skipper Velvet n' Lace #1948.

Hot Pink Flat Buckle Shoes with Silver Buckle, $125
Can be found with Francie Quick Shift #1266, Francie Go Granny Go #1267, and Francie Altogether Elegant #1242.

ANKLE BOOTS

Red Ankle Boots, $20
Can be found with Barbie Shoe Bag #1498, Barbie Night Lighter #3423, Francie Swingin' Skimmy #1264, Skipper Toe Twinkles (pak), and Skipper Some Shoes (pak).

Yellow Ankle Boots, $15
Can be found with Barbie Snap-Dash #1824, Barbie Tunic n' Tights #1859, Barbie Flats n' Heels (pak), Barbie Fashion Accents #1521, Barbie Poncho Put-On #3411, Barbie In Stitches #3432, Francie Zig-Zag Zoom #3445, Francie Cool Coveralls #3281, Skipper Hearts n' Flowers #1945, and Skipper Confetti Cutie #1963.

Royal Blue Ankle Boots, $45
Can be found with Barbie Shoe Bag #1498, Barbie Foot Lights (pak), Barbie Wild Things #3439, Francie Poncho Bravo (pak), Francie In Step (pak), Skipper Wooly Winner #1746.

Gray Ankle Boots, $15
Can be found with Barbie Snug Fuzz #1813, Barbie Shoe Bag #1498, Barbie Foot Lights (pak), and Francie Quick Shift #1266.

Hot Pink Ankle Boots, $20
Can be found with Barbie Stacey Stripes Are Happening #1545, Barbie Foot Lights (pak), Francie Pink Lightning #1231, Skipper Real Sporty #1961, Skipper Quick Changes #1962, Skipper Knit Bit #1969, Skipper School's Cool #1976, Skipper Toe Twinkles (pak), and Skipper Some Shoes (pak).

Orange Ankle Boots, $15
Can be found with Barbie Flats n' Heels (pak), Barbie Fashion Accents #1521, Francie Orange Zip #1548, and Skipper Skimmy Stripes #1956.

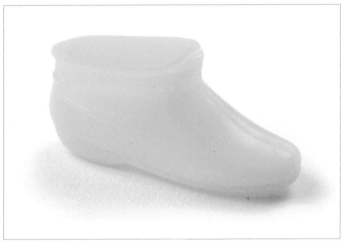

Lime Green Ankle Boots, $15
Can be found with Barbie Trailblazers #1846.

Green Ankle Boots, $15
Can be found with Barbie Shoe Bag #1498, Francie Gad-Abouts #1250, Francie Foot-Notes (pak), Francie Hill Riders #1210, Francie The Combination #1234, Skipper Toe Twinkles (pak), and Skipper Some Shoes (pak).

Kelly Green Ankle Boots, $15
Can be found with Barbie Shoe Bag #1498, Francie Gad-Abouts #1250, Francie Foot-Notes (pak), Francie Hill Riders #1210, and Francie The Combination #1234.

Black Ankle Boots, $65
Can be found with Francie Orange Cozy #1263 and Francie Groovy Get-Up #1270.

White Ankle Boots, $95
Can be found with Skipper Glad Plaids #1946

LACE-UP BOOTS

White Lace-Up Boots with Red Stitching, $35
Can be found with Barbie Fashions n' Sounds Country Music #1055.

Brown Lace-Up Boots, $15
Can be found with Barbie Fashions n' Sounds Festival Fashions #1056 and Barbie Hot Togs #1063.

Green Lace-Up Boots, $15
Can be found with Barbie Fashions n' Sounds Groovin' Gouchos #1057 and Barbie Shoe Scene #3382.

Red Lace-Up Boots, $15
Can be found with Barbie Cold Snap #3429 and Barbie The Short Set #3481.

Yellow Lace-Up Boots, $45
Can be found with Francie Peach Plush #3461.

Honey Gold Lace-Up Boots, $15
Can be found with Barbie Fun Fur #3434 and Barbie Shoe Scene #3382.

White Lace-Up Boots, $10
Can be found with Barbie Kitty Kapers #1062, Barbie Furry n' Fun #3336, Barbie Shoe Scene #3382 Barbie O-Boy Corduroy #3486, and Francie Simply Super #3277.

Navy Blue Lace-Up Boots, $20
Can be found with Barbie Mainly For Rain #3338.

Gray-Brown Lace-Up Boots, $45
Can be found with Barbie Suede n' Fur #3491.

Rose Pink Lace-Up Boots, $75
Can be found with Barbie Fashions n' Sounds Groovin' Gouchos #1057 and Francie Change Offs #3460.

MAJORETTE BOOTS

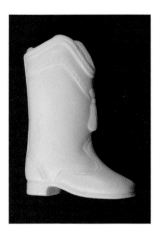   

White Majorette Boots, $20
Can be found with Barbie
Drum Majorette #875.

**Light Blue with Green Stripe
Majorette Boots, $15**
Can be found with Barbie
Now Wow! #1853 and
Barbie Shoe Bag #1498.

Black Majorette Boots, $15
Can be found with Barbie
Fashion Feet (pak).

**Light Blue Majorette Boots,
$15**
Can be found with Francie
Corduroy Cape #1764

RAIN BOOTS

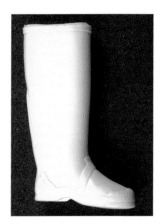   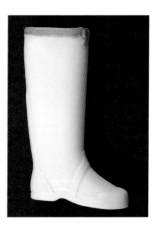

White Rain Boots, $10
Can be found with Barbie
Rain Coat #949, Barbie
Stormy Weather #949,
Barbie Red For Rain #3409,
and Skipper Rain or Shine
#1916.

Yellow Rain Boots, $10
Can be found with Barbie
Fashion Feet (pak).

Orange Rain Boots, $20
Can be found with Barbie
Drizzle Dash #1808, Barbie
Plush Pony #1873, and
Barbie Fiery Felt #1789.

**White Rain Boots with Pink
Trim, $25**
Can be found with Francie
Leather Limelight #1269 and
Francie Foot-Notes (pak).

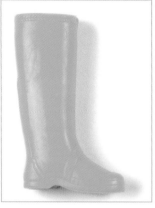

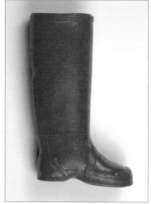

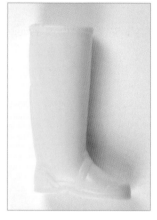

Aqua Rain Boots, $15
Can be found with Barbie Shoe Bag #1498, Barbie Goodies Galore #1518, Skipper Warm n' Wonderful #1959, and Skipper Happy Times (pak).

Red Rain Boots, $15
Can be found with Barbie Super Scarf #3408, Francie Polka Dots & Rain Drops #1255, Skipper Long n' Short Of It #3478, Skipper Nifty Nickers #3291, Skipper Some Shoes (pak).

Note: Some Rain Boots have a molded bow trim.

BALLET SLIPPERS

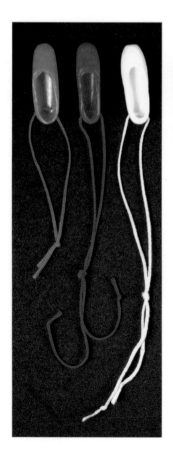

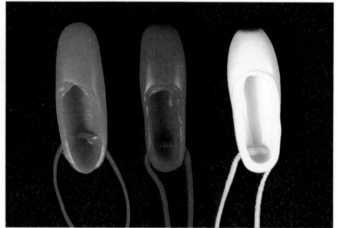

Hot Pink Ballet Slippers, $10
Can be found with Barbie Shoe Bag #1498, Barbie Goodies Galore #1518, Barbie Action Accents #1585, Barbie Prima Ballerina #1787, and Francie In Step (pak).

Red Ballet Slippers, $10
Can be found with Barbie Fashion Feet (pak).

White Ballet Slippers, $10
Can be found with Barbie Ballerina #989 and Skipper Ballet Class #1905.

Pale Pink Ballet Slippers, $15
Can be found with Skipper Ballerina #3471.

RIDING BOOTS

Brown Riding Boots, $45
Can be found with Barbie Riding In The Park #1668.

Orange Riding Boots, $25
Can be found with Barbie Made For Each Other #1881 and Francie Furry-Go-Round #1296.

Black Riding Boots, $35
Can be found with Skipper Learning To Ride #1935.

Red Riding Boots, $45
Can be found with Barbie Smasheroo #1860.

Pink Riding Boots, $35
Can be found with Barbie Shoe Bag #1498, Barbie Walking Pretty (pak), and Francie Culotte-Wot? #1214.

Black Ski Boots, $10
Can be found with Barbie Ski Queen #948.

SKI BOOTS

Black Ski Boots, $10
Can be found with Ken Hunting Shirt (pak), Ken Ski Champion #798, Ken Going Hunting #1409, and Ken Shoes For Sports (pak).

Fuchsia Ski Boots, $25
Can be found with Barbie Action Accents #1585.

Navy Blue Ski Boots, $10
Can be found with Ken Ski Scene #1438.

Orange Ski Boots, $15
Can be found with Barbie The Ski Scene #1797.

Snow Boots

Red Snow Boots, $20
Can be found with Skipper Sledding Fun #1936.

Hot Pink Snow Boots, $15
Can be found with Barbie Shoe Bag #1498, Skipper Flower Showers #1939, and Skipper Goin' Sleddin' #3475.

Yellow Snow Boots, $20
Can be found with Skipper Action Fashion (pak).

Courreges Boots

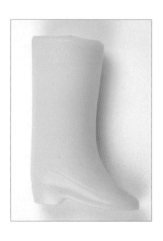

Yellow Courreges Boots, $15
Can be found with Barbie Anti-Freezers #1464, Twiggy Original Outfit, and Francie Snake Charmer #1245.

Clear with Red Trim Courreges Boots, $25
Can be found with Francie Clear Out! #1281, Francie Foot-Notes (pak), and Skipper Toe Twinkles (pak).

Orange Courreges Boots, $25
Can be found with Barbie Shoe Bag #1498, Jamie Furry Friends #1584, and Francie The Wild Bunch #1766.

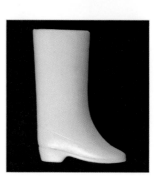

White Courreges Boots, $15
Can be found with Barbie Shoe Bag #1498.

Silver Courreges Boots with Orange Trim, $25
Can be found with Barbie Zokko! #1820.

Red Courreges Boots, $35
Can be found with Jamie Strollin' In Style #1247.

Clear with Orange Trim Courreges Boots, $20
Can be found with Skipper Drizzle Sizzle #1972.

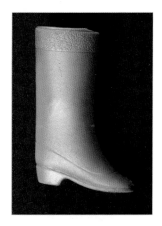

Silver Courreges Boots, $25
Can be found with Twiggy Turnouts #1726.

UNUSUAL BOOTS & SANDALS

Japanese Style Sandals with Attached Socks, $45
Can be found with Barbie In Japan #821.

Orange Roman Sandals Boots, $65
Can be found with Barbie Wild n' Wonderful #1856.

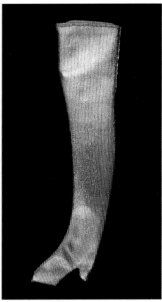

Gold Lamé Thigh High Boots, $65
Can be found with Barbie Winter Wow #1486 and Barbie Golden Groove #1593.

Brown Boots with Zipper, $65
Can be found with Ken Mr. Astronaut #1415.

Brown Boots with Zipper, $65
Can be found with Barbie Miss Astronaut #1641.

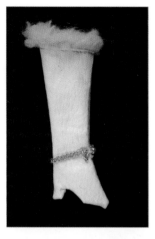

White Textured Vinyl Boots with Gold Chain, $45
Can be found with Barbie Red, White n' Warm #1491.

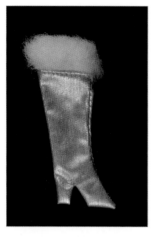

Silver Lamé Boots, $65
Can be found with P.J. Swingin' In Silver #1588.

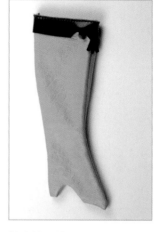

Pink Vinyl Boots with Black Trim, $65
Can be found with Barbie Lamb n' Leather #1467.

Hot Pink Suede Boots, $65
Can be found with Barbie Groovin' Gauchos #1057.

Blue Lamé Thigh High Boots, $65
Can be found with Barbie Maxi n' Mini #1799.

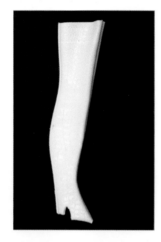

White Textured Thigh High Boots, $65
Can be found with Barbie Wild n' Wintery #3416.

Purple Suede High Boots, $45
Can be found with Barbie Bubbles n' Boots #3421.

Black Shiny Boots with Fuzzy Trim, $65
Can be found with Barbie Magnificent Midi #3418.

Orange Suede Boots with Scalloped Edge, $65
Can be found with P.J. Fashion n' Motion #1508.

Tan Suede Boots with Fringe, $45
Can be found with Barbie Gaucho Gear #3436.

Orange Suede Boots with Fringe, $25
Can be found with Barbie Groovin' Gauchos #1057 and Barbie Fringe Benefits #3401.

Black Textured Spats, $45
Can be found with Francie Fur Out #1262.

White Suede Boots, $25
Can be found with Francie Western Wild (pak).

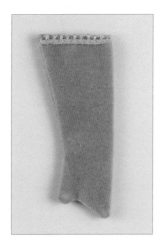

Aqua Suede Boots, $25
Can be found with Francie Western Wild (pak).

Brown Suede Boots, $25
Can Be Found With Francie Western Wild (pak).

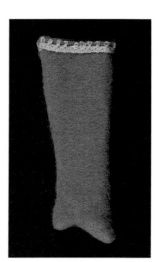

Purple Felt Boots, $25
Can be found with Francie Western Wild (pak).

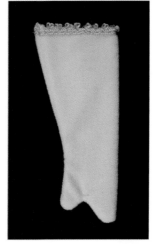

Yellow Suede Boots, $25
Can be found with Francie Western Wild (pak).

Multicolor Floral Sock Boots, $175.
Can be found with Barbie Poodle Doodles #1061.

Cork Sandals with Yellow Ties, $15
Can be found with Francie Cool It (pak).

Cork Sandals with Red Ties, $45
Can be found with Francie Summer Coolers #1292.

Gold Felt Boots, $25
Can be found with Francie Western Wild (pak).

Brown Suede with Pink Cord Lace Up Boots, $85
Can be found with Barbie Festival Fashion #1056.

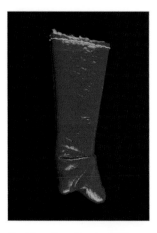

Red Leather Boots, $35
Can be found with Francie
Long On Leather #1769.

**Navy Suede Boots with Red
Trim, $65**
Can be found with Francie
Double Ups #3286.

**Aqua Suede Boots with
White Trim, $20**
Can be found with Francie
Buckaroo Blues #3449.

**Yellow Sandals with Dot
Cut-outs, $45**
Can be found with Skipper
Sunny Suity #1975.

SQUARE TOE SHOES

**Black Square Toe
Shoes with Black
Ribbon, $65**
Can be found with
Barbie Party Lines
#3490.

Hot Pink Square Toe Shoe, $8
Can be found with Francie
Satin Happenin' #1237, Francie
Altogether Elegant #1242,
Francie Pretty Power #1512,
Francie Sunny Slacks #1761,
Francie Pink Power #1762,
Francie The Entertainer #1763,
Francie In Step (pak), Francie
Midi Bouquet #3446, and
Francie Midi Duet #3451.

White Square Toe Shoes, $8
Can be found with Francie
Pony Coat #1240, Francie
Wedding Whirl #1244, Francie
Waltz In Velvet #1768, Francie
In Step (pak), Francie Bridal
Beauty #3288, Francie Red,
White & Bright #3368, Barbie
Fahion Bouquet #1511, Francie
Sweetheart Satin #3361, Barbie
Purple Pleasers #3483, and
Barbie Satin n' Shine #3493.

Black Square Toe Shoes, $8
Can be found with Checker
Chums #3278, Francie Pretty
Frilly #3366, Barbie Long n'
Fringy #3341, Barbie Pants-
Perfect Purple #3359, Barbie
Pleasantly Peasanty #3360, and
Barbie Shoe Scene #3382.

Yellow Square Toe Shoes, $8
Can be found with Francie Pretty Power #1512, Francie The Slacks Suit #3276, Francie Suited For Shorts #3283, Francie Pretty Frilly #3366, and Barbie Shoe Scene #3382.

Light Pink Square Toe Shoes, $8
Can be found with Francie Midi Duet #3451, Francie Pink n' Pretty #3369, and Barbie Shoe Scene #3382.

Red Square Toe Shoes, $8
Can be found with Francie Plaid Plans #1767, Francie In Step (pak), Francie Midi Plaid #3444, Francie With-It Whites #3448, Barbie Regal Red #3217, and Barbie Shoe Scene #3382.

Red-Orange Square Toe Shoes, $10
Can be found with Francie Wild Flowers #3456.

Blue Square Toe Shoes, $8
Can be found with Francie In Step (pak).

Orange Square Toe Shoes, $8
Can be found with Francie Olde Look #3458, Francie Peach Treats #3285, and Barbie Shoe Scene #3382.

Green Square Toe Shoes, $8
Can be found with Francie In Step (pak), Francie Satin Supper #3443, and Barbie Shoe Scene #3382.

Aqua Square Toe Shoes, $8
Can be found with Twilight Twinkle #3459, Barbie Sport Star #3353, Barbie Glowin' Gold #3354, and Barbie Shoe Scene #3382.

Light Blue Square Toe Shoes, $125
Can be found with Francie Smashin' Satin #3287.

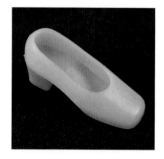

Butterscotch Square Toe Shoes, $25
Can be found with Barbie Golden Glitter #3340.

Royal Blue Square Toes Shoes, $10
Can be found with Barbie Glowin' Gold #3354.

SKIPPER SHOES

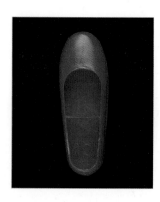

Red Skipper Shoes, $10
Can be found with Skipper Red Sensation #1901, Skipper Day At The Fair #1911, Skipper Cookie Time #1912, Skipper Platter Party #1914, Skipper Ship Ahoy #1918, Skipper School Girl #1921, Skipper Can You Play? #1923, Skipper What's New At The Zoo? #1925, Skipper Chill Chasers #1926, Skipper Dog Show #1929, Skipper Patent n' Pants #1958, Skipper Shoe Parade (pak), Francie Hi-Teen #1272, Skipper On Wheels #1032, and Skooter Cut n' Buttons #1036.

Black Skipper Shoes, $10
Can be found with Skipper Silk n' Fancy #1902, Skipper Town Togs #1922, Skipper Rainy Day Checkers #1928, Skipper All Spruced Up #1941, Skipper Shoe Parade (pak), and Francie Checker Chums #3278.

Black Skipper Shoes with Yellow Pompon, $35
Can be found with Skipper Masquerade #1903.

White Skipper Shoes, $10
Can be found with Skipper Flower Girl #1904, Skipper Dress Coat #1906, Skipper Me n' My Doll #1913, Skipper Outdoor Casuals #1915, Skipper Land and Sea #1917, Skipper Happy Birthday #1919, Skipper Junior Bridesmaid #1934, Skipper Popover #1943, Skipper All Prettied Up #1949, Skipper Shoe Parade (pak), and Skipper Party Time #1021.

Green Skipper Shoes, $10
Can be found with Skipper Right In Style (green version) #1942, Skipper Young Ideas #1513, Skipper Shoe Parade (pak), and Skipper Bright and Breezy #1590.

Pink Skipper Shoes, $10
Can be found with Skipper Sunny Pastels #1910, Skipper Country Picnic #1933, Skipper Rolla Scoot #1940, and Skipper Shoe Parade (pak).

Royal Blue Skipper Shoes, $10
Can be found with Skipper Fun Time #1920 and Skipper Shoe Parade (pak).

Yellow Skipper Shoes, $10
Can be found with Skipper Tea Party #1924, Skipper Beachy Peachy #1938, and Skipper Shoe Parade (pak).

Aqua Skipper Shoes, $10
Can be found with Skipper Perfectly Pretty #1546, Skipper Let's Play House #1932, Skipper Right In Style (blue version) #1942, Skipper Shoe Parade (pak), Francie Land Ho! #1220, and Skipper Bright n' Breezy #1590.

Light Blue Skipper Shoes, $10
Can be found with Skipper Let's Play House #1932 and Skipper Shoe Parade (pak).

Black Squishy Skipper Shoes, $20
Can be found with Skipper School Days #1907.

Orange (Taiwan) Skipper Shoes, $20
Can be found with Skipper Trim Twosome #1960, Skipper Pants n' Pinafore #1971, Skipper Fancy Pants (blue version) #1738, Skipper Double Dashers #3472, Skipper Some Shoes (pak), and Skipper Sporty Shorty (pak).

Light Blue (Taiwan) Skipper Shoes, $15
Can be found with Skipper Jeepers Creepers #1966, Skipper Fancy Pants (blue version) #1738, and Skipper All Over Felt #3476.

Lime Green (Taiwan) Skipper Shoes, $15
Can be found with Skipper Plaid City #1977, Skipper Lot's Of Lace #1730, Skipper Young Ideas #1513.

Yellow (Taiwan) Skipper Shoes, $20
Can be found with Skipper Chilly Chums #1973, Skipper Eeny Meeny #1974, Skipper Daisy Craizy #1732, Skipper Twice As Nice (yellow version) #1735, Skipper Some Shoes (pak), and Skipper Very Best Velvet #1586.

White (Taiwan) Skipper Shoes, $15
Can be found with Skipper Velvet Blush #1737, Skipper Pink Princess #1747, Skipper Dressed In Velvet #3477, Skipper Sweet Orange #3465, Skipper Tennis Time #3466, Skipper White, Bright n' Sparkling #3374, and Skipper Some Shoes (pak).

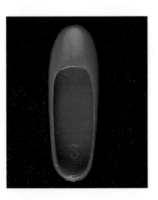

Blue (Taiwan) Skipper Shoes, $15
Can be found with Skipper Hopscotchins #1968, Skipper Rik Rak Rah #1733, Skipper Twice As Nice (blue version) #1735, and Skipper Red, White n' Blues #3296.

Hot Pink Squishy (Taiwan) Skipper Shoes, $15
Can be found with Skipper Lolapaloozas #1947, Skipper Posy Party #1955, Skipper Budding Beauty #1731, Skipper Party Pair #3297, and Skipper Toe Twinkles (pak).

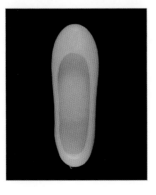

White Squishy Skipper Shoes, $15
Can be found with Skipper Ice Cream n' Cake #1970.

Red (Taiwan) Skipper Shoes, $15
Can be found with Skipper Super Slacks #1736, Skipper Turn Abouts #3295, Skipper Flower Power #3373, and Skipper Toe Twinkles (pak).

Gold (Taiwan) Skipper Shoes, $25
Can be found with Fluff Sunshine Special #1249.

Aqua (Taiwan) Skipper Shoes, $15
Can be found with Skipper Triple Treat #1748, Skipper Young Ideas #1513, and Skipper Toe Twinkles (pak).

Tan Skipper Shoes, $25
Can be found with Barbie Live Action Original Outfit #1155.

Blue Skipper Shoes with Blue Strap, $125
Can be found with Francie Totally Terrific #3279.

Royal Blue (Taiwan) Skipper Shoes, $15
Can be found with Skipper Toe Twinkles (pak) and Skipper Some Shoes (pak).

Wooden Clog Shoes for Barbie, $20
Can be found with Barbie In Holland #823.

Wooden Clog Shoes for Ken, $20
Can be found with Ken In Holland #777.

Black Slipper Shoes, $45
Can be found with Barbie Little Red Riding Hood and The Wolf #880.

Gold Slippers, $25
Can be found with Barbie Arabian Nights #874.

Red Velvet Slippers, $20
Can be found with Barbie Guinevere #873.

Green Velvet Slippers, $20
Can be found with Ken The Prince #772.

Red and Gold Slippers, $25
Can be found with Ken Arabian Nights #774.

Brown Zippered Astronaut Boots for Ken, $75
Can be found with Ken Astronaut #1415.

Brown Zippered Astronaut Boots for Barbie, $75
Can be found with Barbie Astronaut #1641.

Red Bow Shoes, $8
Can be found with Tutti Tutti Skippin' Rope #3604.

Black Bow Shoes, $8
Can be found with Tutti Clowning Around #3606.

Orange Bow Shoes, $8
Can be found with Tutti Cookin' Goodies #3559, Chris Original Outfit #3570, and Tutti Plantin' Posies #3609.

Hot Pink Bow Shoes, $20
Can be found with Chris Fun Timers #3301, Pretty Pairs Lori n' Rori Original Outfit #1133, and Pretty Pairs Nan n' Fran #1134.

White Bow Shoe, $8
Can be found with Tutti Original Outfit #3550, Tutti Melody In Pink #3555, Tutti Swing A Ling #3560, Tutti Ship Shape #3602, Tutti Come to My Party #3607, Tutti Let's Play Barbie #3608, Tutti Sea Shore Shorties #3614, and Tutti Flower Girl #3615.

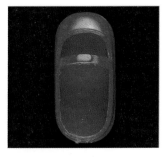

Red Sneaker, $10
Can be found with Todd Original Outfit #3590, Tutti Walkin' My Dolly #3552, Tutti Sundae Treat #3556, and Tutti Skippin' Rope #3604.

White Sneakers, $8
Can be found with Tutti Me and My Dog #3554 and Tutti Sundae Treat #3556.

White Strap Shoes, $8
Can be found with Tutti Original Outfit #3580, Tutti Melody In Pink #3555, Tutti Swing A Ling #3560, and Tutti Birthday Beauties #3617.

Red Strap Shoes, $8
Can be found with Tutti Sand Castles #3603 and Tutti Skippin' Rope #3604

Red Sneakers with White Bottom, $15
Can be found with Buffy and Mrs. Beasley Original Outfit #3577.

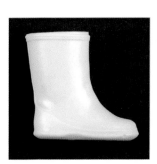

Short White Boots, $10
Can be found with Chris Fun Timers #3301 and Tutti Puddle Jumpers #3601.

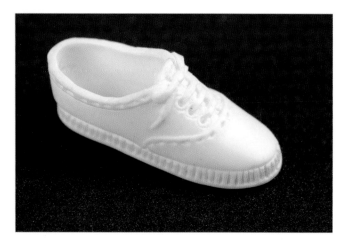

White Tennis Shoes, $10
Can be found with Barbie Tennis Anyone? #941, Barbie Fashion Feet (pak), Barbie Candy Striper Volunteer #889, Barbie Outdoor Life #1637, Barbie Tennis Team #1781, Barbie Good Sports #3351, Barbie Overall Denim #3488, Francie Sportin' Set #1044, Francie Tennis Tunic #1221, and Francie Ready! Set! Go! #3365.

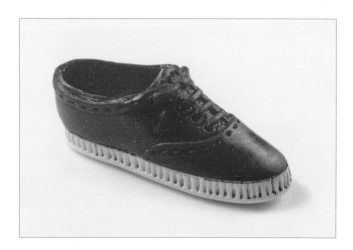

Red Tennis Shoes with White Bottoms, $20
Can be found with Barbie Cheerleader #876 and Barbie Fun At The Fair #1624.

Red Tennis Shoes, $35
Can be found with Barbie The Zig Zag Bag #3428.

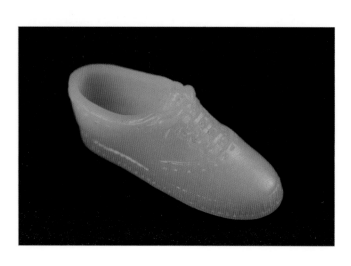

Aqua Tennis Shoes, $20
Can be found with Barbie See-Worthy #1872, Barbie Golfing Greats #3413, and Francie Right for Stripes #3367.

Barbie Doll Accessories #923 NRFB $275

Purse Pak NRFB $175

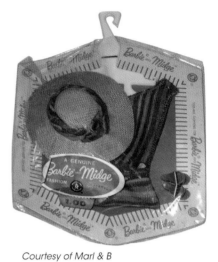

Courtesy of Marl & B

Knit Accessories NRFB $225

Courtesy of mcmastersandharris.com

Shoe Wardrobe NRFB $275

Courtesy of Marl & B

For Barbie Dressmakers NRFB $35

For Rink And Court NRFB $75

Courtesy of Marl & B

**Costume Completers
NRFB $145**

Courtesy of Marl & B

Dress Up Hats NRFB $75

**Fashion Accents NRFB
$175**

Courtesy of mcmastersandharris.com

**Color Coordinates NRFB
$125**

Courtesy of mcmastersandharris.com

**Barbie's Boudoir #1834
$125**

Leisure Hours NRFB $125

Courtesy of Marl & B

Fashion Feet NRFB $100

Courtesy of Marl & B

Match Mates NRFB $150

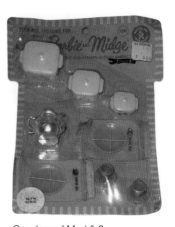

Courtesy of Marl & B

Set N' Serve NRFB $175

Courtesy of Marl & B

Glamour Hats NRFB $175

Courtesy of Julie Delong

Flats N' Heels NRFB $175

Courtesy of Marl & B

Have Fun NRFB $150

Courtesy of mcmastersandharris.com

Kitchen Magic NRFB $175

Courtesy of mcmastersandharris.com

Cook Ups NRFB $175

Courtesy of mcmastersandharris.com

Fancy Trimmins NRFB $125

Courtesy of Vicki Mueller

Finishing Touches NRFB $125

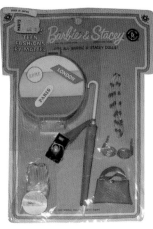

Courtesy of Marl & B

Tour Ins NRFB $125

Sears Exclusive NRFB $175
Goodies Galore #1518.

Courtesy of Marl & B

Sears Exclusive NRFB $175
Fashion Accents #1521.

All The Trimmings NRFB $125

Walking Pretty $100

Accessories Pak for Ken & Allen

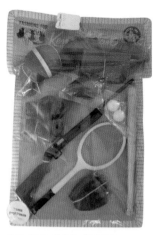

Courtesy of Julie Delong

Sportsman NRFB $125

Courtesy of Sheryy Baloun

Dr. Ken's Kit NRFB $150

Courtesy of Marl & B

Top It Off NRFB $75

Courtesy of Marl & B

Ken Accessories Pak $50

Courtesy of Marl & B

Party Fun NRFB $175

Courtesy of Marl & B

Best Foot Forward NRFB $75

Courtesy of Sheryy Baloun

Golf Gear NRFB $50

Shoes For Sports NRFB $75

Shoe Ins NRFB $50

Just For Fun NRFB $75

Courtesy of Julie Delong

Shoe Parade NRFB $125

Hats N' Hats NRFB $75

Courtesy of Marl & B

Beauty Bath NRFB $125

*Courtesy of Kevin Mulligan from
Joeslist.com*

Action Fashion NRFB $75

Happy Times NRFB $75

Side Lights NRFB $75

Courtesy of Marl & B

Mod Hatters NRFB $150

Courtesy of Marl & B

Hair Do's NRFB $125

Footnotes NRFB $150

**For Francie Dressmaker
NRFB $50**

In Step NRFB $125

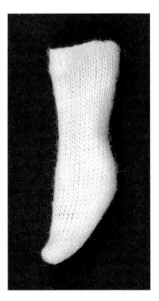

White Cotton Knit Sock, $15
Can be found with Barbie Tennis Anyone? #941, Barbie Cheerleader #876.

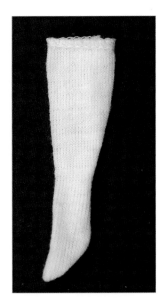

White Cotton Knit Knee High Sock, $25
Can be found with Barbie Little Red Riding Hood And The Wolf #880.

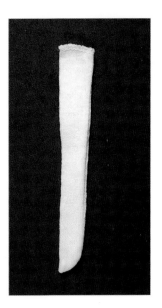

White Cotton Knit Thigh High Sock, $25
Can be found with Barbie in Holland #777.

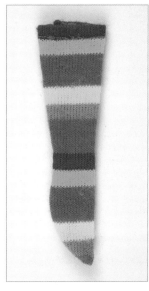

Multicolored Striped Knit Knee High Sock, $75
Can be found with Barbie Stripes Are Happening Gift Set For Stacey #1545.

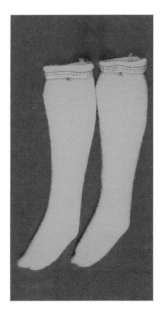

Aqua Cotton Knit Sock With Gold Braid, $35
Can be found with Barbie Sea Worthy #1872.

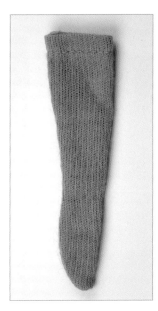

Aqua Cotton Knit Knee High Sock, $25
Can be found with Barbie Golfing Greats #3413.

Pink and White Checked Nylon Knee Sock with Strap, $45
Can be found with Busy Talking Steffie original outfit #1186.

Olive Green Thigh High Sock, $125
Can be found with Barbie Hot Togs #1063.

Olive Green Thigh High Sock, (left) $25
Can be found with Francie Quick Shift #1266

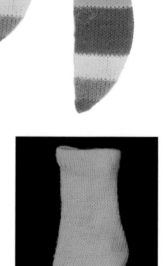

Red Cotton Knit Sock, $10
Can be found with Ken Campus Hero #770, Ken Accessory Pak, Ken Going Huntin' #1409, Ken Victory Dance #1411, Ken Campus Hero 1964 #770, Ken Best Foot Forward Pak, Ken White Is Right Pak, Ken Seein' The Sights #1421, Ken Seein' The Sights #1421, Ken A Go Go #1423.

Stripe Cotton Knit Sock, $10
Can be found with Ken Casuals #782, Ken Casuals 1964 #782, Ken Best Foot Forward Pak.

Olive Green Knee High Sock, $15
Can be found with Ken Sport Shorts #783.

Yellow Cotton Knit Sock, $15
Can be found with Ken Dreamboat #785, Ken Accessory Pak, Ken Best Foot Forward Pak.

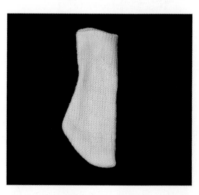

Black Cotton Knit Sock, $10
Can be found with Ken Saturday Date #786, Ken Army And Air Force #797, Ken Special Date #1401, Ken American Airlines Captain #779, Ken Best Foot Forward Pak, Ken Rovin Reporter #1417, Ken Best Man #1425, Ken Big Business #1434, Ken Here Comes The Groom #1426, Ken Best Man #1425.

Black Nylon Sock, $15
Can be found with Ken Tuxedo #787, Ken And Barbie Trousseau Set #864.

White Cotton Knit Sock, $15
Can be found with Ken Time For Tennis #790, Ken The Yachtsman #789, Ken Boxing Pak, Dr. Ken #793, Ken Sailor #796, Ken Drum Major #775, Ken The Yahtsman 1964 #789, Ken Best Foot Forward Pak, Ken Morning Workout Pak, Ken Going Bowling #1403, Ken Hiking Holiday #1412, Ken Holiday #1414, Ken Jazz Concert #1420, Ken Mountain Hike #1427, Ken Fabulous Formal #1595, Ken Guruvy Formal #1431.

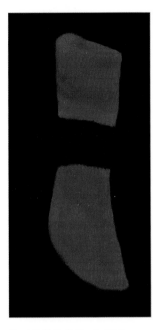

Red Tall Knit Sock With Navy Stripe, $25
Can be found with Ken Touchdown #799.

Red Tall Knit Sock, $25
Can be found with Ken Play Ball #792.

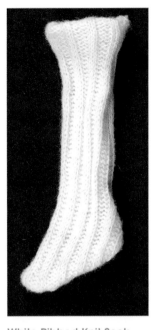

White Ribbed Knit Sock, $20
Can be found with Ken In Switzerland #776.

Tan Knit Sock, $20
Can be found with Ken Army And Air Force #797.

White Cotton Knit Knee High Sock, $20
Can be found with Ken in Holland #777.

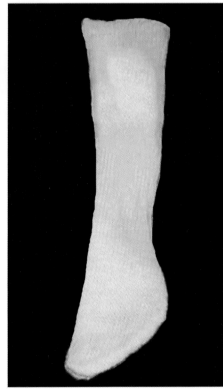

Brown Cotton Knit Sock, $45
Can be found with Ken
College Student #1416

Olive Cotton Knit Sock, $50
Can be found with Ken
Summer Job #1422

Red Knit Sock, $15
Can be found with Ken Play
It Cool #1433

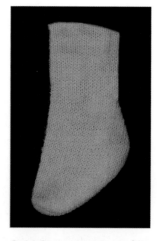

Gold Cotton Knit Sock, $15
Can be found with Ken
Bold Gold #1436

Gold Tricot Sock, $15
Can be found with Ken The Skiing Scene#1438, Ken The Suede
Scene #1439, Ken Slacks Are Back Pak, Ken Brown On Brown
#1718

Black Tricot Sock, $15
Can be found with Ken V.I.P. Scene #1473, Ken Slacks Are Back
Pak, Ken Midnight Blues #1719

Burgundy Tricot Sock, $15
Can be found with Ken The Night Scene #1496, Ken Slacks
Are Back Pak, Ken Denims For Fun #3376, Ken Cool N' Casual
#3379

Blue Tricot Sock, $15
Can be found with Ken Slacks Are Back Pak, Ken Casual Cords
#1717

Blue Cotton Knit Sock, $15
Can be found with Ken
Town Turtle #1430, Ken
Casual All Stars #1514, Ken
Red, White and Wild #1589,
Ken The Sea Scene #1449

Orange and Yellow Knee High Sock, $20
Can be found with Francie Mini Chex #1209

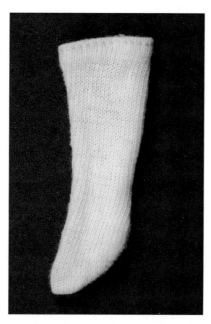

Yellow Cotton Knee High Sock, $15
Can be found with Francie Twiggy-Do's #1725, and Barbie Snap Dash #1824

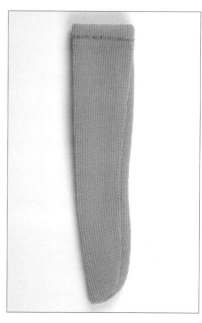

Pink Nylon Knee High Sock, $20
Can be found with Francie Sissy Suits #1228

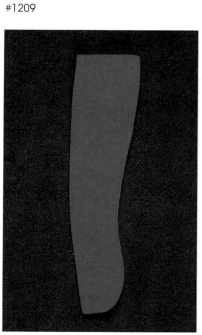

Hot Pink Nylon Knee High Sock, $35
Can be found with Francie Little Knits #3275

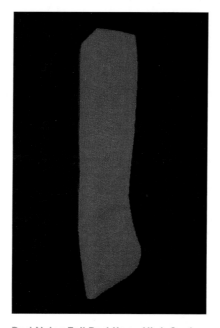

Red Nylon Tall Red Knee High Sock, $35
Can be found with Francie Checker Chums #3278

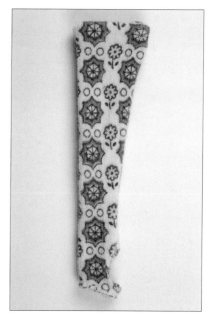

Multicolored Knee High Sock with Strap, $50
Can be found with Francie Suited For Shorts #3283

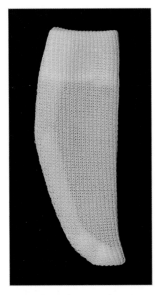

Short Nylon White Sock, $10
Can be found with Skipper Red Sensation #1901, Silk N' Fancy #1902, Flower Girl #1904, Sunny Pastels #1910, Me N' My Doll #1913, Ship Ahoy #1918, Happy Birthday #1919, School Girl #1921, Junior Bridesmaid #1934, Right In Style #1942, Velvet N' Lace #1948

Yellow Ribbed Knee High Sock, $25
Can be found with Skipper Hearts N' Flowers #1945

Orange, Pink, and Green Multi Colored Knit Knee High Sock, $20
Can be found with Skipper Skimmy Stripes #1956

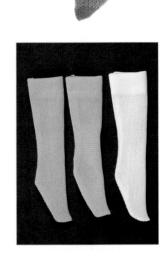

Pink or White Nylon Knee High Sock, $15
Can be found with Skipper School Days #1907

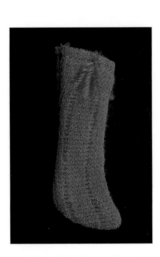

Hot Pink Knit Knee High Sock with Orange Tassel, $20
Can be found with Skipper Quick Changes! #1962

Turquoise and Yellow Knit Knee High Sock, $65
Can be found with Skipper Confetti Cutie #1592

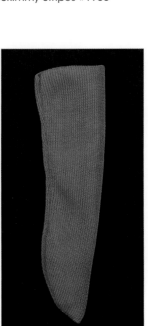

Hot Pink Tricot Knee High Sock, $10
Can be found with Skipper Knit Bit #1969, Skipper Daisy Crazy #1732

Yellow and Pink Daisy Knee High Sock, $15
Can be found with Skipper Daisy Crazy #1732

Dark Blue Cotton Knee High Sock, $25
Can be found with Skipper Wooly Winner #1746

Green Cotton Knee High Socks, $35
Can be found with Skipper Young Ideas #1513

Red Knit Knee High Sock, $35
Can be found with Skipper Play Pants #3292

Red Tricot Knee High Sock, $25
Can be found with Skipper Red, White N' Blues #3296

RICKY

Red Cotton Knit Sock, $15
Can be found with Ricky Saturday Show #1502, Ricky Sunday Suit #1503, Ricky Let's Explore #1506.

Red Cotton Knit Sock with Navy Band, $15
Can be found with Ricky Little Leaguer #1504.

White Cotton Knit Sock, $20
Can be found with Skateboard Set #1505.

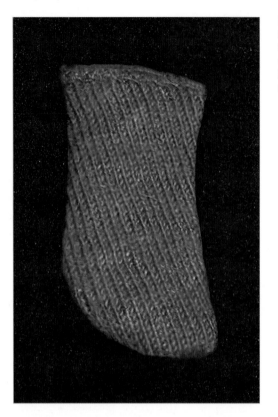

Blue Cotton Tall Sock, $25
Can be found with Todd Sundae Treat #3556.

Blue Cotton Knit Sock, $20
Can be found with Todd original outfit #3590.

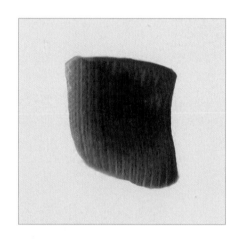

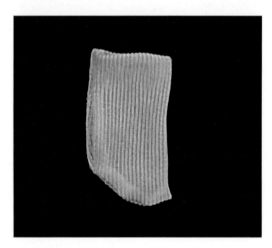

White Tricot Sock, $20
Can be found with Tutti Walkin' My Dolly #3552, Tutti Night, Night, Sleep Tight #3553, Tutti Melody In Pink #3555, Tutti Sundae Treat #3556, Tutti Cookin' Goodies #3559, Chris Fun Timers Gift Set #3301, Buffy and Mrs. Beasley #3577, Pertty Pairs Lori and Rori #1133, Tutti Ship Shape #3602, Tutti Come To My Party #3607.

Yellow Tricot Sock, $45
Can be found with Tutti Swing-A-Ling #3560.

Courtesy of mcmastersharris.com

Prong Stand, $850-1000
Can be found with Ponytail
Barbie 1959 #850.

**Wire Stand with TM Pedestal
Base, $150-200**
Can be found with Ponytail
Barbie 1959–60 #850

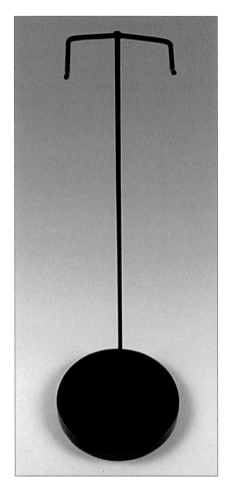

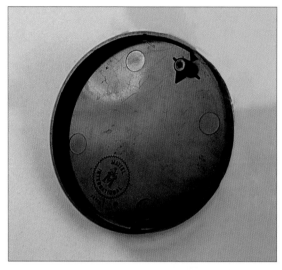

**Wire Stand with R Pedestal
Base, $150–200**
Can be found with Ponytail
Barbie 1960 #850.

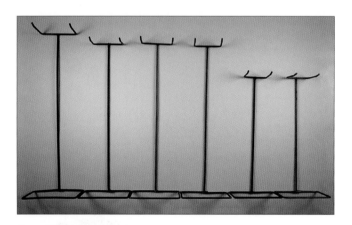

From left to right
Ken, Barbie Black, Barbie Gold, Francie, Ricky, Skipper.

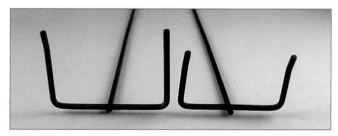

*Barbie left side, Francie right
side*

Barbie Black Wire Stand, $25
Can be found with Ponytail
Barbie #850, Bubble Cut
Barbie #850, Fashion Queen
Barbie #870.

**Barbie or Midge Gold Wire
Stand, $25**
Can be found with Barbie
Swirl Ponytail #850, Miss
Barbie #1060, Barbie
American Girl #1070, Midge
Gift Set #1160, Midge #860,
Midge #1080.

**Ken or Allan Black Wire
Stand, $20**
Can be found with Ken #750,
Ken #1020, Allan #1000, Allan
#1010.

Francie Gold Wire Stand, $65
Can be found with Francie
#1160, Francie #1130.

Ricky Black Stand, $25
Can be found with Ricky
#1090.

**Black Skipper or Skooter
Stand, $25**
Can be found with Skipper
#950, Bendable Leg Skipper
#1030, Skipper Re-Issue #950,
Skooter #1040, Bendable Leg
Skooter #1120.

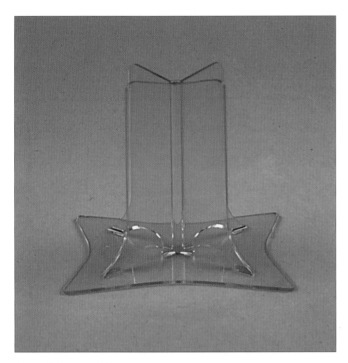

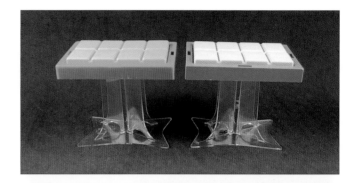

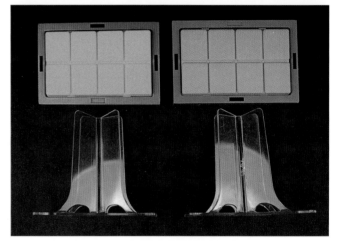

Clear X Stand, $20

Can be found with Standard Barbie #1190, Twist N' Turn Barbie #1160, Barbie Trade In Box Version #1160, Twist N' Turn Flip #1160, Talking Barbie #1115, Dramatic Living Barbie #1116, Living Barbie #1116, Hair Happenin's Barbie #1174, Barbie with Growing Pretty Hair #1140, Busy Barbie with Holdin' Hands #3311, Talking Busy Barbie #1195, Montgomery Ward Ponytail Barbie #3210, Busy Steffie with Holdin' Hands #3312, Talking Busy Steffie #1186, Talking Busy Ken #1196, Busy Ken with Holdin' Hands # 3314, Francie Twist N' Turn #1170, Black Francie #1100, Francie Hair Happening's Francie #1122, No Bangs Francie #1170, Short Flip Francie #1170, Growing Pretty Hair Francie #1129, Busy Francie #3313, Busy Francie with Holdin' Hands #3313, Francie Rise N' Shine #1194, Twist N' Turn Skipper #1105, Dramatic New Living Skipper #1117, Dramatic Living Skipper #1117, Casey #1180, Twiggy #1185, Talking P.J. #1113, Twist N' Turn #1118, Stacey #1165, Talking Stacey #1125, Stacey #1165, Twist N' Turn Christie # 1119, Talking Christie #1126, Brad #1114, Jamie #1132, Julia #1127, Talking Julia #1128, Truly Scrumptious #1108, Talking Truly Scrumptious #1107.

Clear X Stand with Pink Box Top Stool, $35

Can be found with Talking Barbie Clear box #1115.

Clear X Stand with Green Box Top Stool, $35

Can be found with Talking Christie Clear box #1126.

Touch N' Go Stand, $25

Can be found with Barbie Live Action #1155, Live Action Ken #1159, Live Action P.J. #1156, Live Action Christie #1175

Light Blue Stand Stage, $75

Can be found with Barbie Live Action #1152

Pink Blue Stand Stage, $75

Can be found with P.J. Live Action #1153

Blue Stand Stage, $75
Can be found with Ken Live Action #1172.

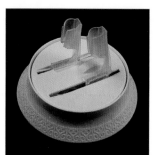

White Walking Stand, $25
Walk Lively Miss America #3200.

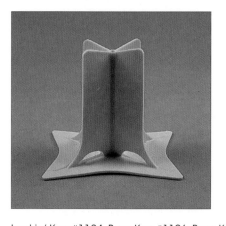

White X Stand, $15
Can be found with Busy Barbie With Holdin' Hands #1182, Talking Busy Barbie #1195, Growin' Pretty Hair Barbie #1144, Jamie Strollin' In Style #1247, Busy Ken With Holdin' Hands #3314, Mod Hair Ken #4224, Quick Curl Barbie #4220, Talking Ken #1111, New Good Lookin' Ken #1124, Busy Ken #1196, Busy Ken with Holdin' Hands #3314, Quick Curl Francie #4222, Quick Curl Skipper #4223, Quick Curl Kelley #4221, Miss America #3194, Quick Curl Miss America #8867.

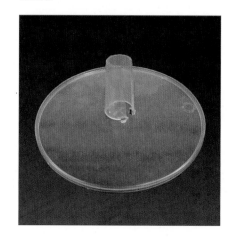

Clear Pose N' Play Two Piece Stand, $15
Can be found with Living Fluff #1143, Sunshine Special Gift Set for Fluff #1249.

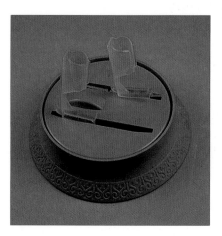

Tan Walking Stand, $25
Can be found with Walk Lively Barbie #1182, Walk Lively Ken #1184, Walk Lively Steffie #1183.

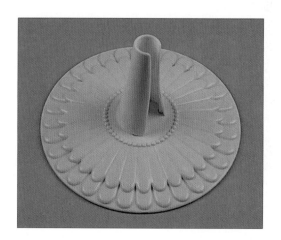

Can be found with Barbie Ballerina 1975 #9093.

Pink and Blue Wig Stand, $35
Can be found with Color Magic Color N' Curl
Set #4093.

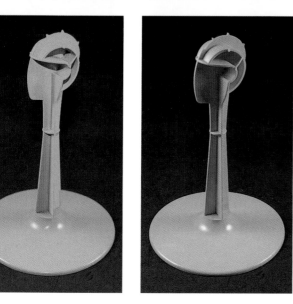

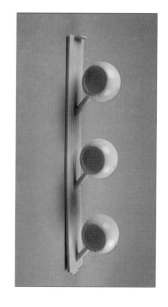

White Wig Stand, $15
Can be found with Fashion Queen Barbie #870, Miss Barbie #1060, Barbie Wig Wardrobe #0871, Midge Wig Wardrobe # 1009.

Can be found with Color Magic Fashion.

White Fashion Mannequin, $15
Can be found with Sew Magic 1973 #8670.

KEN® IN MEXICO Ken and Barbie® were in sunny Mexico on September 15, the night of Mexico's biggest "fiesta" (festival). This is like our 4th of July; Mexicans celebrate with fireworks and dancing! Barbie gave Ken a sombrero! This broad-brimmed, high-crowned hat is worn by almost all Mexicans. Some Mexicans carry lunch in the crown of the sombrero...others use it for a water bucket for their burros! Do you know how Ken used his sombrero? At the fiesta, he and Barbie danced around it, doing the Mexican Hat Dance!

SAVE AND TRADE MATTEL® TRAVEL PICTURES: Barbie in Holland, Ken in Holland, Barbie in Hawaii, Ken in Hawaii, Barbie in Switzerland, Ken in Switzerland, Barbie in Mexico, Ken in Mexico and Barbie in Japan!

(Back)

Ken in Mexico Travel
Picture Pamphlet, $25

(Front)

Barbie in Japan Travel
Picture Pamphlet, $25

BARBIE® IN MEXICO Barbie will never forget Mexico! The friendly people ...the sunny weather...the fun she and Ken® had at a "fiesta" (festival). Ken gave Barbie a lovely black lace mantilla (man-tee-ya)...a veil Mexican women wear over their heads. Though mantillas look delicate, many a time a mantilla served as a rope for a lover to climb up a balcony to steal a kiss from his love! Barbie decided to wear *hers* to formal parties.

SAVE AND TRADE MATTEL® TRAVEL PICTURES: Barbie in Holland, Ken in Holland, Barbie in Hawaii, Ken in Hawaii, Barbie in Switzerland, Ken in Switzerland, Barbie in Mexico, Ken in Mexico and Barbie in Japan!

(Back)

Barbie in Mexico Travel
Picture Pamphlet, $25

(Front)

Barbie in Hawaii
Travel Picture
Pamphlet, $25
Ken in Hawaii
Travel Picture
Pamphlet, $25

(Front)

KEN® IN SWITZERLAND On her
very first day in Switzerland, Barbie®
wore her Swiss costume. Ken told her
that she looked charming...just like a
Swiss teen-ager! Barbie wanted to
get a special souvenir of Switzerland for
Ken, so she wandered through the shops. She saw the Swiss
making chocolate...and cheeses...and watches. She had a
hard time trying to decide what to get him. But finally she
found just the thing...a souvenir pipe, a long one just like
Swiss men smoke, to go with Ken's Swiss costume!

*SAVE AND TRADE MATTEL® TRAVEL PICTURES: Barbie in Holland,
Ken in Holland, Barbie in Hawaii, Ken in Hawaii, Barbie in Switzerland,
Ken in Switzerland, Barbie in Mexico, Ken in Mexico and Barbie in Japan!*

(Back)

Barbie in Switzerland Travel
Picture Pamphlet, $25

Ken in Switzerland Travel
Picture Pamphlet, $25

Ken in Switzerland Travel
Picture Pamphlet, $25

KEN®IN HOLLAND Ken loves to "clomp"
around in his wooden shoes. Wooden shoes are
called "*Klompen*" in Holland! Even today
the Dutch wear wooden shoes after floods or
rain. Since no one is allowed in the house
wearing klompen, it was easy for Barbie®
and Ken to tell how many people there were in a household
simply by counting the pairs of wooden shoes at the door!

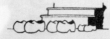 How many children do you think
there are in this house? How
many adults?

*SAVE AND TRADE MATTEL® TRAVEL PICTURES: Barbie in Holland,
Ken in Holland, Barbie in Hawaii, Ken in Hawaii, Barbie in Switzerland,
Ken in Switzerland, Barbie in Mexico, Ken in Mexico and Barbie in Japan!*

(Back)

Ken in Holland Travel Picture
Pamphlet, $25

Barbie in Holland Travel
Picture Pamphlet, $25

(Front)

Barbie & Ken Red Riding Hood And The Wolf Theatre Program, $25

Barbie Arabian Nights Theatre Program, $25

Ken Arabian Nights Theatre Program, $25

Barbie Cinderella Theatre Program, $25

Ken The Prince Theatre Program, $25

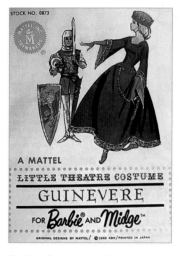

Barbie Guinevere Theatre Program, $25

Ken King Arthur Theatre Program, $25

223